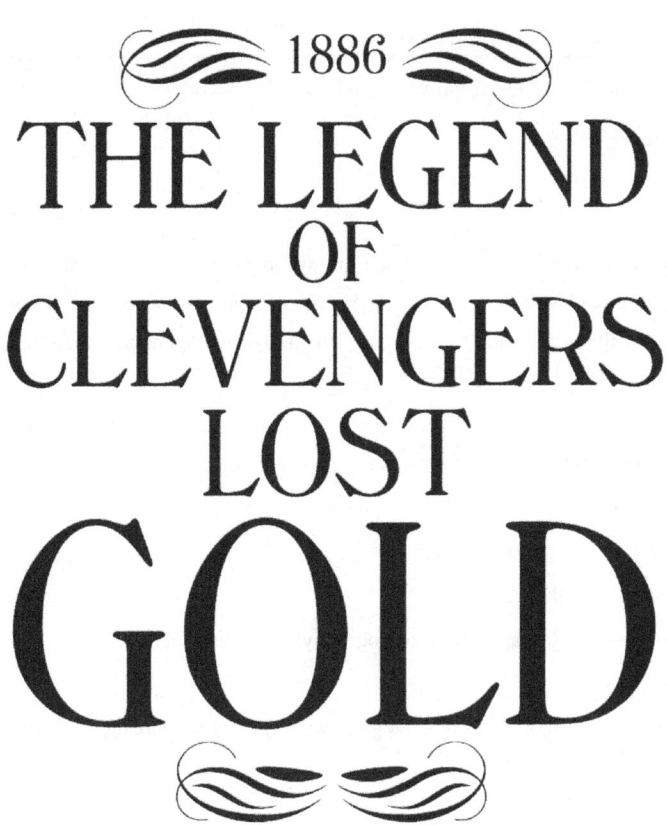

1886
THE LEGEND OF CLEVENGERS LOST GOLD

with Linda Gatewood

The Legend of Clevengers Lost Gold

Copyright © 2018 by Aaron Werner / Linda Gatewood
All rights reserved.

No part of this publication may be reproduced, stored in a retrieval system or transmitted in any way by any means, electronic, mechanical, photocopy, recording or otherwise without the prior permission of the author except as provided by USA Copyright Law.

Published in the United States of America

    ISBN-13:978-1721031917
    ISBN-10:172103191X
    Non-Fiction/ Biography & Autobiography/Historical/ General

Cover design copyright © 2018 by Grzegorz Japoł (grzegorz.japol@gmail.com)

Acknowledgment

I would like to thank the people who helped me in my efforts to put together this book. Thank you to Linda Gatewood, the author of six published novels, who is also my mother. She fell in love with this story the moment she heard it, spending a tremendous amount of time assisting in researching, writing and editing for all to enjoy.

I would like to thank the staff at Sharlot Hall Museum and the Arizona State Library, Archives and Public Records that worked with me on request after request for historical photographs and records of the court services, county documents and other important information that I gathered.

I would like to thank all the veteran treasure hunters that have inspired so many people around the world to join in the hunt for lost treasure. One in particular is Stephen Shaffer who mentored me along this journey. He truly is the real deal and I find it fortunate to be able to walk the dusty trails with him

Most of all I want to thank my family who participated in the creation of this book by not just providing feedback and material but also participating in the hunt.

We hope your family will have as much enjoyment as ours searching for Clevenger's Lost Gold.

*Dedicated to my wife **Angela** and our two children, **Jordan** and **Emmarysa** who have allowed me to discover the most valuable treasure in the world... **family!***

Book Chapters

Chapter One	*Pulling Up Roots*
Chapter Two	*New Territory*
Chapter Three	*The Massacre*
Chapter Four	*Jessie's Story*
Chapter Five	*The Trial*
Chapter Six	*After the Hanging*
Chapter Seven	*The Treasure Map*
Chapter Eight	*Looking for Gold*
Chapter Nine	*The Journey*
Chapter Ten	*Contradictions*
Chapter Eleven	*Lost and Found Treasures*
Chapter Twelve	*Secret of Clevenger's Gold*

Preface "The Legend"

In the Buckskin Mountains just 15 miles southeast of Kanab, Utah is a lost treasure that has never been found. This book is the first of its kind, documenting the factual details of this lost treasure. If you believe this is an old treasure hunt from years past, that thousands have searched for, you can think again. If you think this treasure has already been found, you are mistaken.

The legend of Clevenger's lost gold of 1886 is a true story that is well documented and legally substantiated. The reporters of many popular newspapers in Southern Utah and Northern Arizona of that time kept the details in the headlines for months. They reported every aspect, interviewing the parties involved, and wrote about their findings. It was a headline grabber: *Clevengers Murdered for their Riches!* For example, the Deseret News headlines proclaimed, *"A Shocking Murder: Interesting Details of the Horrible Death and the Capture of the Perpetrators!"* The Weekly Champion printed, *"Paid the Penalty, The One Taken and The Other Left."* The Arizona Weekly stated, *"The Sentence; Wilson and Johnson to be Hanged Friday, August 12th."*

> **THE SENTENCE**
>
> Wilson and Johnson to Be Hanged Friday, Ausust 12th.

E1

Newspaper after newspaper kept up with the events and reported them on the front page. The trail leading to the spot where the gold was lost is painstakingly tracked and details provided, but the buried treasure was never officially reported as being found.

The ruthless murder of Samuel and Charlotte Clevenger was considered at one time to be one of the most brutal acts ever committed in the territory of Arizona. The killings were senseless and unnecessary, committed for greed and revenge. Even though the murderers were hunted down and punished for the crime, there are still unanswered questions about the legitimacy of their testimonies, the veracity of events and most important, the true motive for such a heinous act.

While doing research on this lost treasure, I found a dearth of actual proof acknowledging the location of the missing wealth, but what missing treasure ever has a map in which "X" marks the spot? There is so much evidence that points to the existence of a good amount of money that has never been accounted for, and that makes this worthy of a closer examination.

The various accounts of the crime contrast in numerous ways and I want to present all of them. Some of the details differ according to who is giving testimony. I have presented all that are relevant, even though they are sometimes dissimilar. Other accounts, I've been able to research and combine the stories to match. Wading through the speculation that was present in 1886, I will let you choose what you believe are the facts.

In a day and age where communication consisted of a telegraph in only the largest cities and towns, many locations had none whatsoever. The popular mode of transportation was horse and buggy. The railroad had reached the west, but only ran to the most accessible cities, leaving the smaller communities dependent on the trustworthy, but slow and uncomfortable, horse. Any kind of travel consisted of long-term planning, little luggage and great risk.

The risk involved was the travel isolation and possibility of outlaws on the loose. The stagecoaches hired men to serve as guards who carried rifles to protect the people and contents of the carriage. Pioneers traveled in groups as added protection against all sorts of danger, from wild animals to rogue Indians of that time. Lone travelers had to depend on themselves for protection against all threats. Knowing who to trust with your life was a constant contention and those who chose unwisely, paid the price.

The amount of lost money is verified to be approximately $2,000 to as much as $6,000 in currency, silver and possibly some gold. By today's standards, the value of this lost treasure is worth much more, possibly as much as one million dollars. At that time, the currency in use was commonly silver certificates, which in today's market can bring a great return. An 1886, $1 silver certificate was recently estimated to be worth $15,000 - $20,000. Most people are familiar with the current value of silver and gold, so any discovery of a cache of these coins would be a windfall!

The story is intriguing and full of mystery. There are questions still unanswered. During the investigation covered by many newspapers, the people involved in this crime would consistently change their statements and testimonies, except maybe one person, and even she kept a deep dark secret for many years.

To understand the mystery we need to understand the people who created this incredible true story of intrigue. I want to walk you through their lives as accurately as possible with what little information is available. Piecing together the events, the personalities and the actions of those involved, I hope to paint a picture as close to the truth as can be conceived. By combining historical events of that period and the many newspapers, court papers, and testimonies, I hope to add the missing pieces.

In this book, I would like to follow the trail of the treasure – where it first started, where it traveled, and approximately, where it ended up.

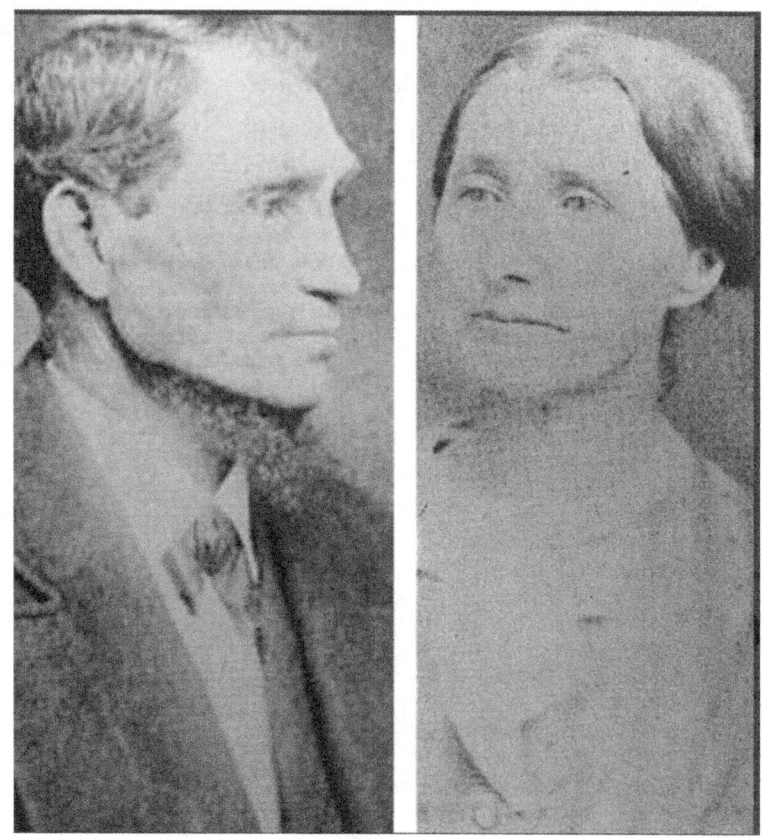

E2: Samuel and Charlotte Clevenger

Pulling up Roots

Samuel Clay Clevenger (1831-1886) and Charlotte (Brown) Clevenger (1831-1886) were in their mid-fifties when this story began. He was born in North Carolina but by the time he was 23 years old, he was living in Hamilton, Indiana, where he met and married Charlotte Brown on January 24, 1854.

The Civil War raged between the years of 1861-1865 and Samuel Clevenger enlisted as a Volunteer Union Soldier and held the rank of Private in the Illinois 154th Regiment.

They had no children, but adopted a girl named Jessie at the age of two, who was born about 1873. Charlotte's health was deteriorating and she may have needed more care than her husband alone could provide.

Due to her health issues, they moved to the Fort Thomas, Arizona area. For those of you who have never been there, it's among a group of small settlements along Highway 70 in the Gila Valley, dotted by agriculture and pioneer history, and about 143 miles east of Phoenix, AZ.

The early Native Americans who populated this area knew how to survive on the bare necessities in that part of Arizona. Their knowledge of wild foods, seasonal fare and wild game provided them with all their needs. In the hot, dry climate, there were years of drought. During those times, many Indians died of starvation and malnutrition. They depended on the land for their sustenance. When the water disappeared, so did the animals. Without streams and rivers, the fish were gone, too. It wasn't a popular place for settlers, but many tried anyway.

The earliest military presence in that location was former Camp Goodwin, constructed in 1864 and named for Arizona's first territorial governor, John N. Goodwin. Its beginnings were hampered and the camp was abandoned after a short time due to failed buildings and malaria from a nearby spring.

In 1876, the current site of the community was chosen as a "new post on the Gila," selected to replace Camp Goodwin. Initially, the site was named Camp Thomas in honor of Civil War Major General George Henry Thomas. Until 1882, the area would be known by several names including Clantonville, Camp Thomas, Maxey and finally, Fort Thomas.

Mrs. Clevenger's health was poor and according to some newspaper reports, she suffered from tuberculosis. The husband and wife had followed their physician's advice to move to a warmer climate. The Arizona desert, especially along the Gila, promised warmer, dry days. After two years, they tired of the relentless heat, the parched earth and yearned for a new start in a different place. Charlottes' health was fragile and the journey would be difficult for her, but she supported her husband in this new venture.

Even though they were considered elderly in those days, both in their mid-fifties, they were known for being hard working and industrious. In the spread-out, sparsely inhabited valley, they had many friends who wished them well on their undertaking.

According to different accounts, in March and possibly as early as February of 1886, Mr. Clevenger, who had a reputation for being a testy old man and was most commonly referred to as "old man Clevenger", concluded to sell his place and all his stock along the San Pedro in Arizona. He reportedly sold his ranch and in addition, sold his water rights to his neighbor Mr. Jerome B. Collins and planned to move his family into the Washington Territory, where it is believed he was going to start a new ranch.

He and his wife had an adopted daughter, Jessie, who is described in various newspapers as being either fourteen, fifteen or seventeen years old – depending on what source – at the time of the relocation. Her official age according to a census dated 1880 (six years before the murders) displayed her full name as Jessie May Clevenger from Missouri, age seven years old, making her thirteen or fourteen at the time of the murders.

It is interesting to note that there is a land patent filed in 1857 in Palmyra, Missouri, where Samuel acquired 80 acres of land (paid in full). It is possible that during his time in Missouri, little Jessie would have been born and eventually adopted by Samuel & Charlotte Clevenger in 1875.

Old man Clevenger reserved one span of horses with harness, and packed up a wagon, cooking outfit and their bedding. From the sale of his property, it is believed he received $2,150.00 and pocketed an extra $500 from the sale of his water and ditch rights. Clevenger's ditch was about eight or nine miles from Fort Thomas according to a deed dated January 12th 1886. It was used as an irrigation ditch providing much needed water to the area.

Some reports claim that he also received a number of horses – 28 to 35 – in trade that he herded northward toward the Washington Territory.

It was also mentioned in The Clifton Clarion 15th of Dec. 1886 that "Clevenger had with him some $6000 in money."

> Several months ago, Samuel Clevenger his wife, and adopted daughter, a young white man and a negro, started from Apache county, intending to go to Washington Territory. Clevenger had with him some $6,000 in money, between 30 and 40 mules and horses, etc, etc. Lately, Clevenger's remains were found near the Utah line, in the northern part of Yavapai county.

E3: *The Clifton Clarion 15th of Dec., 1886*

The amount of money that Clevenger carried on his journey is debated in several records. We know he had $500 from the sale of his water and ditch rights, as stated in the county records. The outlaws admitted stealing that cash and all the horses. It isn't widely known how much he received from the sale of his ranch that he was taking with him for a new start. One article reported that he received $2,000 and yet another, $6,000. Without the deed of sale, we can't know for sure, but we can find out what his property was worth from the tax records of 1884. "2 houses, furniture, improvements on ranch near Camp Thomas, 37 cattle, 3 horses, 2 mules, 2 wagons, harness, saddle, Misc. all valued at a total $2,174. This value almost doubles when sold, ($4,348 and possibly as high as $6,000) so taking into account some assets traded in horses, we can assume he was carrying with him a good amount of money.

An interesting note about Jerome B. Collins, he was known for establishing the notorious town of Maxey near Camp Thomas in June of 1880. Unfortunately he too was murdered 2 months after the Clevenger's by a ranch hand named Williams, possibly related to an individual Collins had killed several years before.

Conflicting accounts say that in late February or early March 1886, he left the San Pedro area with his family as they set out on the long journey to the Washington Territory. The dust blew around the wagon wheels as the team dug their feet deep into the hardened dirt road. The sky was just becoming light with one of those beautiful Arizona sunrises, when the older couple, with all their goods, traveled away to a new venture.

Accompanying them was one of Clevenger's hired hands who had worked on the ranch when it sold. John A. Johnson was given the duty to do chores around the camp, take care of the team and help manage the herd of horses in return for his grub and transportation to Washington Territory. He was also seeking a new life, far from the dust and heat of the Fort Thomas barracks.

Mr. Johnson was born in Trenton, New Jersey and raised in Baltimore. He came to the territory with the 10th Cavalry, stationed along the Gila. This cavalry formed by black men, and named Buffalo Soldiers by the Indians, began duty in Arizona in 1885

E4: *Buffalo soldiers of the 25th Infantry, some wearing Buffalo robes, Ft. Keogh, Montana, 1889*

The 10th Cavalry made great sacrifices while fighting for freedom in the Civil War with nearly 180,000 blacks who served. At the end of the war, they were allowed to enlist in the regular army during peacetime, and were assigned to the American West. There were 3 companies (C, F, and G) in Fort Thomas. Johnson had been discharged from the Fort in February 1886, prior to coming to work for the Clevenger's. He was eager to find a new place to settle after five years of service in the Cavalry, part of it in the hot, dry territory of Arizona.

Taking a job with Samuel Clevenger for no pay whatsoever except food and transportation hints at how anxious Johnson was to escape the Gila Valley.

John Johnson, being a military man, was strong and healthy, and accustomed to long hours of hard work. He would understand dedication and fortitude after his stringent training. He would expect a certain degree of deference and courtesy from others. He pledged to give his time and effort to Mr. Clevenger on the journey, only expecting respect in return.

When the migrant party was complete and outfitted for the long journey ahead, they never looked back. The days ahead were mild, not yet hot at this time of year. The length of their journey would depend on the weather, the road, and the various trails they would need to follow to reach their destination. Providing food and water for the horses would determine where they stopped along the way and how long they stayed. Clevenger would have expected his hired hand to work around the clock, driving the herd of horses, feeding and watering them along the way and helping with the camp each evening when they stopped. Most of the heavy-duty jobs would be done by Johnson as they moved across the territory.

The San Pedro area was dusty and dry with bright green scrub brush dotting the countryside. As they traveled across the sandy road, the view didn't change much. The sky above was a stark blue with hardly a cloud to blemish its expanse. When the wind was still, the journey was easier, but if the dust began to stir because of northerly winds, the sky could quickly disappear into a cloud of dirt. Each day the travelers looked forward to reaching areas that were more established where they could resupply and rest.

One of the more populous cities they were planning to stop at was Phoenix, Arizona, and they were approximately a hundred-forty three miles from there. With good conditions, they figured they should make it by mid-month.

Old Man Clevenger pushed his party to move on every day, without stopping for a prolonged rest. This part of the trail was gentler on the stock. No high mountains to climb, no rivers to ford and the road was clear. The goal was to reach Phoenix and then rest up before continuing into less familiar trails. The Clevenger's were familiar with this part of the trip, having made possible trips into Phoenix over the last two years. Charlottes' poor health possibly warranted a few trips to visit qualified doctors who might be able to heal her.

Each night, they would stop at sunset, feed and water the horses before cooking a meal on the campfire and retiring. Early in the morning, they would be ready to pull out on the trail for another day, just as the sun began to rise. Samuel Clevenger was a hard worker and between him, his adopted daughter, Jessie and Johnson, they were able to manage the journey so far without interruption. It is important to note that if traveling by wagon and oxen a party could accomplish up to 10 miles a day in distance but when traveling with a span of horses, the party could accomplish twice that. They moved swiftly along their journey.

Jessie was the main caregiver for the ailing Mrs. Clevenger and saw to all her needs. She helped her to dress each day, and fulfilled her needs. In addition to those duties, she also cooked the meals for the group. The adopted daughter always made sure that Charlotte ate something, even when the sick lady's appetite was absent.

Jessie worked hard each day, doing chores and fulfilling her mamma's needs, but old man Clevenger never spared a kind word for her. In fact, if she was tardy or if she dissatisfied him in any way, he wouldn't hesitate to reprimand her with a hard hand. He was strict and hard hearted in his way, and little Jessie was his main target. If she earned a whipping, then that was what she got. Even though she was beyond being a child, moving quickly into womanhood, she was at the awkward age for a young girl. Too young to be treated as an adult, yet, too old to be coddled like a child. Girls grew up faster in those days, some ready for marriage by the age of 15, so I imagine Jessie as being about that age, and working as hard as any adult.

The road they were traveling was used by others including the mail carriers and stagecoach. It wasn't unusual to pass by someone who was going the opposite way. Many times, when they stopped for a night, they would find themselves sharing accommodations with others who were also on the move. Access to water and other camping necessities designed the few sheltered camping sites. This was a good way to hear the news of what was going on in places everywhere.

Oftentimes, newspapers were traded and shared among travelers, allowing people to keep up with the times. In the year of 1886, there were plenty of current affairs to share as the first telephone company opened in Phoenix that year and the famous Phoenix Opera House was completed. One small note, on May 8th1886, a Pharmacist named Dr. John Stith Pemberton invented a carbonated beverage that would be named Coca-Cola.

It wasn't unusual to run into people who knew the same folks, had mutual relatives, or were familiar with previous neighbors and towns folks. There was a general feeling of safeness when others shared the road, especially if you shared a connection of similar acquaintances. Many times, a sheriff traveled along with his deputies in search of outlaws. This tendered a safer journey for all.

Samuel C. Clevenger, his wife, adopted daughter, Jessie, and the hired hand, moved across southern Arizona with no incidents and soon arrived safely in Phoenix, the county seat of newly established Maricopa County, created in 1871. This area was part of the New Mexico Territory, designated as such after the Mexican-American war had ended in 1848.

They planned to spend several days there, to rest up the team, and restock their supplies. With this design in mind, they drove out to the Orlando Allen ranch that was located two miles outside of Phoenix on the Wickenburg road, and stayed for three days.

C.T Rogers and Orlando Allen had a large herd of cattle in the Big Chino Valley (an area that the Clevenger's would soon be traveling through). They were known in the area as cattlemen, and attracted talented hired hands to assist with their cattle. The road to Wickenburg passed by the Allen Ranch and was the general direction that they would follow on their journey into Utah before traveling up to Washington Territory. Wickenburg was the first town established in what is now Maricopa County in 1863 and at the time had about 130 people living in it. It would be the second major community the Clevenger's would have traveled through on their journey.

During this time period it was common practice to conceal money in a money belt. More than likely, Samuel Clevenger carried a portion of his money in this manner. The money belt contained the $500 he received from the sale of his water and ditch rights. The bulk of his money, received from the sale of his other holdings, ($2,150-$6,000), is believed to have been secretly tucked into a baking soda can which was hidden inside a satchel and disguised as household items. This was concealed inside the wagon. He carried a rifle to make sure his money was safe and he was ornery enough to use it without much provocation.

While they were camped at the Orlando Allen ranch, Samuel Clevenger and John Johnson ran into an old acquaintance, a man named Frank Wilson who may have been assisting Orlando with the care of his cattle. Hard working cowboys were necessary and shrewd cattlemen were always looking for a good hand. The cattle business was booming and herds were ever expanding. The need for experienced help was constant.

Wilson was a presentable person, in his mid-thirties, with a courteous demeanor. While visiting with Clevenger, he learned that they were traveling into unknown territory and were seeking information about the best route to take, as well as hiring more help to drive their stock north. John Johnson was a military man, experienced in many ways, but he felt he needed another man to assist with driving the large herd of horses on such a long journey.

Frank Wilson gained the confidence of Samuel Clevenger and offered to assist them in their journey in return for board and transportation to Washington Territory. It's possible that Frank Wilson was looking for an opportunity to high tail it out of town for some unknown reason. In 1885 Wilson was accused of stealing a horse from the United States Military.

"After an examination order was made by F.W. Greg, Commissioner of the District Court of the United States- for the first Judicial District of the Territory of Arizona, Frank Wilson was to be held to answer upon the charge of having in his possession, with intent to convert to his own use, property of the United States; one horse furnished and to be used for the Military service of the United States at Graham County in said District, on or about the 9th day of December, A.D. 1884, and whereas bail has been fixed in the sum of $500 for the said Wilson to appear and answer said charge." - UNITED STATES OF AMERICA First Judicial District of Arizona.

Wilson had been indicted in Graham County for horse stealing and ordered to pay $500 to the United States. It was Samuel Clevenger who stepped in on January 26, 1885 and helped him out of that scrape by agreeing to act as sureties or what we might call a bailsman today.

I was not able to verify if this amount was ever paid. It is possible that this was one of the motivations for Wilson's eager departure of the area. It is also possible that Wilson had a debt to Samuel Clevenger and assisting with the move to Washington Territory could possibly be a form of restitution.

On the 17th day of October 1885 Jerome B Collins, the man who purchased Clevenger's property (and who was later murdered) was also charged with violating Section 5438 of the Revised Statutes acknowledging "himself indebted to the United States of America in the sum of $1500, lawful money of the United States, to be levied of his goods and chattels, lands and tenements."

Even more interesting is the fact that Samuel Clevenger himself was charged on the 22nd day of December 1884 and ordered to pay $500 to the United States of America. The date of the crime was on or around the 9th day of December 1884.

"Held to answer upon the charge of having in his possession, with intent to convert to his own use, property of the United States;"

This information was not known until I did the research for this book. It was assumed that Samuel Clevenger and Frank Wilson did not know each other before their journey to the Washington Territory. This recent find not only puts them together two years before the trip north but it also opens the door to the possibility that Frank Wilson and Samuel Clevenger shared a friendship from long before they ever set foot on the path to Washington Territory.

Whatever the reason, he was willing to hire on for no pay at all, with only meals and transportation for the long trip. Since he claimed to know the road well, had experience with driving horses and could guide them along the best route to reach their destination, Wilson joined the group of travelers. Wilson and Johnson both were well known in Fort Thomas as noted in the Clifton Carrier 22nd of December 1886.

He was a welcome addition to the small group, and with the recommendation of his old friend, John Johnson, he settled in and was accepted as a much-needed assistant along the trail.

In those days, there were various different roads and trails through mountain ranges, along riverbanks and into deep valleys. A traveler didn't have a detailed map to follow. Certain roads were marked by mail carriers and the stagecoach, but others offered either a shortcut or easier traveling conditions. If a man had knowledge of these things along with the ability to move cattle or horses to fresh water and feed, he was considered a valuable person to have in a group.

Frank Wilson quickly became this person, charming in all ways; indispensable to old man Clevenger, helpful to the sickly Charlotte and courteous to the young, pretty, Jessie.

New Territory

After several days, the party was ready to resume their trek. The weather had settled down after a fierce windstorm that moved dust from one side of the valley to the other. The unbreathable air had cleared, the dirt was brushed aside and the wagon readied for the journey. After a breathtaking sunset, all was set the next day to start again on the long expedition.

Not only did Wilson offer travel advice, he also worked as hard as the hired hand, John A. Johnson did. They had known each other previously from Fort Thomas and had a good relationship so they worked well together. They were both looking for a new start somewhere in a new place for personal reasons of their own. Everyone was glad to begin again, the wagon and team ready to move out across the desert.

Being in constant contact with one another, it was difficult to keep any secrets. Getting to know your teammates was easy when you lived 24 hours a day with them. There had to be cooperation between them, little complaint and most important of all, ability to do what needed to be done.

Samuel Clevenger had a secret that needed to be kept, especially from the two hired hands. He carried the money belt on his body every day and slept with it tucked under his pillow, next to his rifle. The satchel holding the bulk of his money was guarded carefully in its hiding place inside the wagon. At night, when they pitched tents to sleep in, he carried the satchel inside, carefully disguising it as a clothing container. He cautioned his family to say nothing about it to the other men.

It was rumored, and later reported to various newspapers, that old man Clevenger was on occasion publicly, verbally and physically abusive to his adopted daughter, Jessie. Because of this, the two hired hands resented his treatment of the girl and oftentimes stood up for her. Many times, they witnessed his heavy-handed treatment of the young girl. She was accustomed to the behavior and never defended herself.

When the men interfered in his treatment of Jessie, Clevenger was angry and deeply disturbed by their audacity.

He believed it was nobody's business how he handled his charge.

Jessie always tried to do what her adoptive father wanted, but being young and occasionally distracted, sometimes she just couldn't please him enough. He wouldn't hesitate to knock her down and kick her around to vent his anger. This abuse caused tension between the hired hands and old man Clevenger.

When the group of travelers pulled out of the Phoenix area, they went through Wickenburg, by way of Stanton, and through Peeples Valley. This was a well-traveled road with quant settlements and tidy farms along the way.

They moved through Kirkland Valley, their team and wagon secure, the horses tightly herded, and finally reached Skull Valley. The travelers had heard of this area and the haunted reputation of the valley. Two decades earlier, in 1864, the displaced and starving Yavapai Indians had been warring with the new settlers. The pioneers retaliated by massacring at least thirty-five tribe members at Elbe's ranch in Skull Valley.

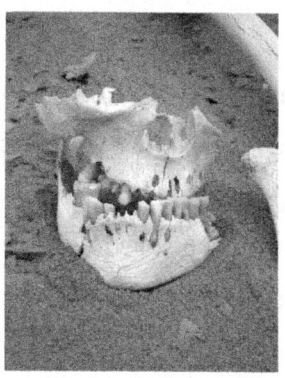

E5: Skull Valley, AZ

Their bodies had joined the numerous bleached bones that already littered the ground. The valley had once been the scene of a great battle between the Yavapai and Pima many years ago before the early explorers came.

Early scouts found the valley covered with human bones and skulls that had lain out in open air for years. During the time when the Cavalry was fighting the Indian Wars, they were criticized because they never buried the dead hostiles after a battle. This was practically impossible because the country was very rocky and they had no suitable tools for this purpose. The bodies were widely scattered over the terrain where they lay. (Credit for information: Prescottazhistory.blogspot.com by Drew Desmond)

After moving on through Skull Valley, they traveled to Tonto Springs and Williamson Valley. The post office was called Simmons at Williamson Valley, so they stopped there to get a supply of grub. The team of horses who pulled the heavy wagon would sometimes need a day's rest before hitching up again.

This travel route was a little longer than the traditional route up through Holbrook but made sense considering the threat of Indians and the number of horses Samuel and his team were moving. It was territory that Frank Wilson was familiar with if he had spent time working with Orlando and his cattle in the Big Chino Valley. Wilson performed well as a guide and with Johnson's help, made sure the horses were well cared for with proper watering, feed and rest.

After restocking, they went to Ash Fork by way of Big Chino Valley, then to Flagstaff by way of Spring Valley. The days were long, but the terrain was interesting, if not challenging. There were few mountains to climb, and the trails led around the large hills that dotted the land, providing an easy route. The heat of each day was tempered by the winds that sometimes blew strong. If a storm ensued, the travelers had to seek what shelter they could, corralling the horses.

Jessie Clevenger wanted to go by the way of Prescott, as she wanted to see the little mountain town that was popular even in that day. Their guide, Frank Wilson said, "No, there is no use pulling that mountain to Prescott and going that far out of the way when we have a direct road over here and no mountain to climb."

Old man Clevenger liked the logical sound of this and agreed with Wilson to bypass Prescott. Jessie thought she would never see her little mountain town but little did she know at that time that Prescott would not only be a place that she would spend a considerable amount of time in her near future, but it would be the central location of one of the most riveting events of her life

The trails Wilson chose were less inhabited, less traveled by others and more remote. He knew the land well, and because of this, he chose to travel in areas that were not as convenient but were less populated. Little did Samuel Clevenger know what lay ahead, or that his new guide, Frank Wilson, had an ulterior motive as to why he picked the trails he did.

As the guide on this trip, he could lead the party in any direction he wanted and if Samuel Clevenger questioned his decisions, Wilson could reason with him until he convinced the old man that he was right. This was how Wilson led the group closer to the Washington Territory.

Wilson could have had several reasons for avoiding the settlement of Prescott or for avoiding any settlements at all. It was as if he was hiding from something or someone. The less he was around people, the happier he was.

For some time now, Wilson and Johnson had been having secretive private talks with one another, while they were in camp or riding along the road ahead of the team. It had been noticed that Clevenger wore a money belt with the cash he needed to make this journey. Once, his hired hands watched him reach into the belt and pull out cash to pay for something. The belt was stuffed with money and both Wilson and Johnson speculated as to how much. Having no cash of their own, they envied the old man's stash.

As the days passed, they watched the old man closely. When he lashed out harshly and unreasonably at Jessie, the hired men would sometimes step up to defend her. Clevenger was quick to remind them of their place and to point out how fragile their employment was. His attitude toward Johnson, the black man, probably had prejudicial undertones and would have been hard to endure. Since Johnson and Wilson were old friends, the sting would have bothered Wilson, too.

There was a seething dislike brewing in Wilson and Johnsons' gut against Samuel Clevenger. As the feelings grew, the hired hands began to make plans of their own and they kept their dark secret from the Clevenger family.

With Frank Wilson as a guide, there were no longer any stops made in towns or thickly settled communities. In fact, those places were dodged whenever possible. He always came up with a clever reason why they should take the path less traveled. Clevenger usually agreed as long as the horses were fed and watered. He craved the company of others very little and paid little attention to that aspect of the trip.

When the outfit arrived at Spring Valley, a few miles from Flagstaff, Mr. Clevenger decided to camp a couple days to let the team rest. He also wanted to do some repairs on the wagon. The camp was made at the ranch of Harry Lyons, a longtime hospitable rancher of Spring Valley. There was plenty of feed for the herd of horses and a water well providing water. This was also a good chance for the women to do some laundry and clean out the wagon.

E6: *Flagstaff Arizona Late 1800's*

They rested for four days, letting the team graze well, before moving on to Flagstaff to purchase more grub. It would be a long time before they could resupply, as the next place to find supplies would be either Johnson or Kanab, Utah, a distance of over 200 miles along a mostly unpopulated track.

They crossed the Little Colorado River just north of Leupp at Grand Falls. There were two primary crossings of the

Little Colorado—one at the Grand Falls, and one at Black Falls, a smaller waterfall some 10 miles (16 km) downstream. It was easier to ford the river at the two waterfalls because at that point, it flows over hard bedrock, making the crossing much easier. Once crossed, they took the direct road to Lee's Ferry on the Big Colorado River. The landscape changed drastically from the cooler pines of mountain splendor to the flat red plateaus and endless hills. The red cliffs off in the distance rimmed the horizon and painted the view with varied color. It was only a hint of the glory of the Grand Canyon that lay westward in Arizona. The Canyon at that time was uninhabited with only a few who braved its perpendicular planes and named it a place of wonder.

The ferry was a major link between settlements in Arizona and Utah and wagon loads of early pioneers were ferried across the Colorado River as early as 1870.

They weren't the only wagon with stock crossing the river. There were a few other folks and each had to wait their turn both coming and going. It was a good chance to visit and find out how the trail ahead looked.

The weather was mild and the high winds of last week had settled into a gentle breeze, making the crossing successful. After crossing the river, and facing the unknown road ahead, old man Clevenger started to become suspicious of his hired hands. There was growing animosity between him and the men because of his treatment of the girl, Jessie, and probably, because of his money. Remember, he wasn't paying Wilson and Johnson to help on this journey. All he was doing for them was feeding them and providing them with a horse to ride. Imagine traveling that distance without a penny in your pocket. It was costing Clevenger nothing but a little extra grub to have two highly qualified men, lead, guide, and run stock over thousands of miles of trails, watching over them day and night. The two men were beholden to him for their needs, even as they diligently worked long hours every day for him. If he was ornery and abusive, not only toward Jessie, but toward them also, they would probably resent him and that resentment could grow daily.

Samuel Clevenger was no fool and kept a wary eye focused on his gear, especially the satchel that contained his money. His intuition told him that something wasn't right. He could feel the eyes of those men on him, almost burning a hole through his back. He sharpened his wits and practiced caution. If he didn't need their help, he might have fired them. Since there was no one else he could hire this far out on the track, he would have to make do with those guys. Things might change when he reached Kanab. That might be a good time to give those two fellows the boot.

The area they were traveling in after crossing the Colorado River was new to Clevenger. He had traveled through the eastern part of the US but this was the farthest he'd gone out west. He'd heard of all the land available in the great Washington Territory. The grass was tall and green in that state and water was plentiful. He envisioned a large productive ranch with herds of healthy horses.

After the crossing, Samuel Clevenger started to practice a little ritual each night after dark. He would sneak off by himself, dig a little hole and bury his container of money that he removed from the satchel, returning early before dawn to dig it up. His money was down by $150 after having spent some on supplies. He also had the $500 from the sale of his water rights making his total somewhere between $2,500-$6,000. He always carried the $500 on his person, implying it was all he had for the trip, to those who needed to know. While he buried the pouch of secreted money, Jessie assisted him by watching out and trying to distract the two hired men.

After he returned and they were all bedded down, he would whisper to Jessie where it was buried. He never knew when he might feel a sharp knife between his shoulder blades, even as he slept.

For two nights in a row, as they stopped each evening, the money was successfully buried, unbeknownst to anyone else in the camp. John A. Johnson and Frank Wilson allowed their attention to be focused on the pretty Jessie, while sickly Mrs. Clevenger rested inside the tent, exhausted from the day's travel.

On May 20, 1886, the next camp was made. (Even though the date varies in different accounts, this is the date that the courts settled on.) With Wilson as the guide, they chose an isolated route and the road they camped beside was traveled very little in those days, by anyone, except the mail carrier, who carried mail between Lee's Ferry and Johnson, Utah. Sometimes stockmen who lived in the House Rock Valley and vicinity also used the road.

By now, the travelers were road weary and had spent a total of three months on the trail. They were halfway there and looked forward to settling in on a piece of land in the Washington Territory before winter hit in the late fall.

Only a few people passed them in this sprawling area before they set up camp. One man, Mr. McAlister, later remembered the old couple, the two hired hands and the pretty, adopted daughter. He chatted with the group for a few minutes before he moved on his way.

E7: *Map of Buckskin Mountains (site of missing treasure)*

The Clevenger party camped near the Summit of the Buckskin Mountains where the horses could graze on scrub. They were all tired and finished the evening chores quickly before the hired hand, John A. Johnson, quietly slipped away after it was dark to check on the horses. There was no water up there and the restless horses would have to wait until the next water hole to drink their fill. The scrub would hydrate them until the next day when they reach Navajo Well near modern day Pioneer Gap.

Wilson settled onto his sleeping roll near the wagon as Johnson disappeared into the darkness. Jessie sat beside the hired hand and they visited, while she kept a wary eye out for old man Clevenger to return.

Meanwhile, Samuel Clevenger sneaked away from camp into the surrounding area to bury his money. The area was humming with the sound of locust and the random sound of a bird chirping in the background. After assuring himself that he was alone, he surveyed the large rock on the right hand side of the old road, looking for the perfect spot to hide his loot.

The rock had large pockets in it that often collected rainwater or spring runoff and provided much needed water to the animals in the area. The location Samuel chose to camp at was a popular camping area for cowboys and other travelers that relied on the water from the pockets to rehydrate their livestock. It was about 5 miles south of the Utah border and was in the heart of the Buckskin Mountains.

The ground was hard but only a few feet from the large rock the area contained soft red dirt that was easy to dig. He located his prime spot and dug a hole to hide his precious treasure. Placing a large rock next to his buried stash to serve as a marker, he felt satisfied that this location that would keep his money safe. The $2,000-$6,000 was nearly all currency, mostly one's, ten's, and twenty-dollar bills, but is believed to have contained gold coins and silver pieces. After he finished, Mr. Clevenger trekked back to camp and climbed into the tent where his wife slept. Jessie also settled in the tent to go to sleep. He whispered to Jessie that he'd buried the money beside the big rock by the road. Then he lay down on his bedroll and closed his eyes, his head resting on the pillow that secretly covered the money belt containing the $500.

That night, the Arizona sky was alive with stars. They glittered against the black backdrop of the heavens and gave little light back to earth. The creatures who roamed in the dark instinctively avoided the campsite, their intuition sharp. For just a moment on that dark night, everything suddenly changed for those asleep in their bedrolls. A thought became an action and life was never the same again.

Sometime before the sun rose the next day, while all was quiet without even the chirp of a morning bird, the two hired hands murdered Mr. and Mrs. Clevenger.

The Massacre

The grisly murder scene wasn't examined until five or six months later. One newspaper account states that sometime in the month of October, in the same vicinity, a group of campers on their way to Kanab, Utah had set up camp for the night. While settling in, they made a shocking discovery. A human arm protruded from the ground, having been ravaged by coyotes.

Another account discovered in the files of the office of Arizona's Secretary of State and attached to a petition for the pardon of John A. Johnson, stated the bodies as having been found much earlier. The letter addressed to N.O. Murphy, Acting Governor of Arizona, Phoenix, A.T., dated December 4, 1890, said that a party consisting of Cephas Perkins, a well-known cattleman of Holbrook, was also on the road to Utah. Accompanying him was Mr. and Mrs. Graves. The group had followed the Clevenger's from Lee's Ferry in May, 1886 and camped near the same spot sometime later after the massacre.

Perkins had some loose stock and was running them near Clevenger's camp area one morning when his horse stepped to his knees into a soft spot, stumbled and fell heavily with him. He righted himself and his horse, continued after the stock, but returned later to investigate the hole. He discovered signs of a new grave along with the hand and part of a woman's head. He drove on to Kanab and reported what they had found, then continued on their way to St. George.

Another report attested that the mail carrier, Harry Clayton, discovered the scene in late September. On Clayton's usual trek from House Rock to Johnson, he noticed that the dirt had been disturbed on the top of Buckskin Mountain, about 25 miles southeast of Kanab and 5 miles south of the Utah board. He soon discovered there had been a crime committed as some of the human bones had been exposed. The coyotes or other wild animals had dug up the remains. There was evidence that a fire had been built over the remains but had not consumed the bodies.

Clayton immediately notified the officer at Kanab, who went to the scene of the double murder. Sensing a horrible crime, the officer at once notified the Sheriff of Yavapai

County by mail, as there was no telegraphic communication nearer Prescott at that time, than Flagstaff.

According to the same newspaper account, the coroner Zadok. K. Judd, from Kanab, UT, was summoned along with a coroner's jury to examine the bodies, which were later removed to Kanab and buried in what is believed to be the old northern cemetery. A man who accompanied the jurors, Mr. McAlister, recognized the bodies as the Clevenger's. He remembered them as they traveled in that area the preceding spring, herding a mob of horses. When McAlister had visited with them briefly, Mr. Clevenger had told him he planned to buy a ranch in Washington Territory.

Samuel Clevenger was found partially clothed with two axe wounds to his head, while Charlotte, in her nightclothes, had a solitary wound on her head resembling the backside of an axe. The bodies were buried in a single hole, one on top of the other. There was no sign of Jessie Clevenger or the two hired hands.

In the Salt Lake Herald dated November 11, 1886, it was reported:

A Double Tragedy Man and Woman Murdered on Buckskin Mountain

Some time ago, the Herald published a special dispatch from Kanab in reference to the discovery of the body of a man on the Buckskin Mountains which had been partly unearthed by the coyotes. The dispatch said that the coroner and others would at once go to the scene to hold an inquest, as there was no doubt but that a murder had been committed. It now transpires that the body of a woman was also discovered in the same grave, over which a fire had been built in order to cover the newly disturbed ground. The verdict of the jury that sat on the case has been received and is as follows:

Territory of Utah, County of Kane

An inquest holden in Kanab Precinct Kane county on the 21st day of October A.D., 1886, before Zadok K. Judd, coroner of said county, upon the bodies of two persons unknown, there lying dead (one man and one female) by the jurors whose names are hereunto subscribed. The jurors upon their oaths do say that the deceased came to their death by the blows of an axe in the hands of some person or persons unknown and with felonious intent, as from the nature and locality of the wounds, they were attacked while lying asleep, camping out upon the Buckskin Mountains, their bodies being thrown together in one grave, covered lightly with earth and a large fire built over them, charring the clothing and flesh of the man. The bodies were discovered by passer-by through the coyotes digging into the grave.

In testimony whereof the said jurors have here unto set their hands, the day and year aforesaid.

A.E. Riggs

B.F. Stewart

John B. Elsey

Jurors

Sheriff William (Billy) J. Mulvenon from Yavapai County investigated the crime. At that time, Yavapai County extended from Wickenburg in the south to the Utah line on the north. What is now Coconino County was at that time part of Yavapai County. Horseback or buckboard were the only modes of travel, and in many instances, trips had to be made on horseback because there were no roads. Billy Mulvenon followed the standard of George Ruffner, Bucky O'Neill, Jim Roberts and many of the old time sheriffs, and was suited to the rigors of western life as a lawman. He stayed on course until he got his man.

E8: Sheriff Mulvenon. Courtesy of Sharlot Hall Museum Library & Archives / Leroy E. Eslow Photos / PC-4 7.2

Sheriff Mulvenon carried his Winchester rifle and two Colt single arm six-shooters that always rested firmly on his hips. He'd had them for many years and trusted them in the worst situations. He always hoped he never had to use his weapons, but experience had taught him their necessity and to always be prepared.

He traveled at once from Prescott, the capital of the Arizona Territory, and crossed the Little Colorado River at Grand Falls and then crossed the Colorado River at Lee's Ferry, before riding his horse into the Buckskin Mountains. He was met by the Kanab officers who took him to the location.

At the scene, a thorough investigation revealed to the officers that two white persons had been murdered, but that was all they knew. The remains were carefully removed to Kanab and eventually buried.

Beginning his investigation sometime in late October or November, Mulvenon could find nothing definite as to who the murdered persons were, nor any clue as to who committed the crime. He heard of the identification from Mr. McAlister, the man who accompanied the coroner jurors from Kanab, but didn't consider it proof of identity, although it seemed a reliable lead at the time.

He did hear of two men, one white and one black man, and a white woman, with a four-horse team, going through Kanab several months before the discovery of the bodies. They were recognized by another traveler who had crossed Lee's Ferry in May when the Clevenger party had crossed, and knew there had been two old folks in the party that were missing from the group who were seen passing through Kanab.

As word spread about the discovery of the bodies, people who remembered anything about the group of travelers came forward to help the sheriff track down the killers and find the missing girl.

The sheriff made the hundred-mile trip back to Lee's Ferry to find more information about the Clevenger group when they had crossed the ferry in May. He rode his strong horse that had carried him all over Arizona and brought him safely home each time.

The ferryman, Warren Johnson, convinced his brother-in-law, David Brinkerhoff, to be his partner at the ferry for approximately five years. Brinkerhoff (A Mormon Bishop who was commonly called Bishop Brinkerhoff by locals) was ferryman at that time, and remembered that back in May, an old couple, another man, a black man, and a young girl had camped at his place before crossing the ferry. They had bought hay for the horses and supplies for themselves. They had 28-head of loose horses that they were herding. He also remembered that the old man paid for everything, and that the young woman called him father.

He was able to give a good description of the team and wagon because one of the horses was a little skittish about getting on the ferryboat. The sheriff kept careful notes of all the details. It was part of his job to not miss a thing. The sheriff believed that he'd correctly identified the victims and possibly also the murderers. He had a good idea about the motive for the crime and a scenario of its perpetration.

Even though Mulvenon had ridden his horse four hundred miles already, he rode back to Kanab to gather more information before starting on the trail of the killers.

The ferryman had stated that Clevenger had paid for hay and supplies but there was no money found on the victims. Mulvenon figured the killers must have taken it. He was a dedicated lawman and was ambitious in his pursuit of the perpetrators of the horrific murders. In fact, this crime was being labeled the most brutal in all of Arizona. He couldn't help but feel angry that this had occurred and he was determined to find the guilty parties.

Sheriff Mulvenon was accompanied about one hundred miles into Utah by the Kanab officer. At this point, the officer returned home and Mulvenon made the rest of the trip alone.

Although his horse was one of the best in the country, it was getting very leg weary from carrying a two hundred pound man, saddle, guns and irons, which consisted of two pairs of handcuffs and leg irons. Leaving his horse on excellent feed at a ranch, he purchased a relay. The new horse gave out in less than two hundred miles, as he was soft and not accustomed to hard traveling. The next horse Mulvenon acquired was a little better.

The sheriff wasn't the only one looking for the outlaws who murdered and robbed the Clevenger's. It is believed he had a joint pursuit going on with Sheriff Haskell Jolley of Kane County, UT and traveled by railway to meet up with two of the Kane officers in Pioche, NV where there was evidence that the suspects had been there a while back

E9: Sheriff Haskell Jolly 1884-1887 Kane County

The murderers, along with a young woman, had been spotted in this small gambling town. Since the ferryman at Lee's Ferry had described a young girl being in the party that crossed over, the Sheriff knew her body was not buried along with the old people. Learning that there was a young girl with the outlaws, made the pursuit more intensive and Mulvenon pushed himself forward.

In Pioche, they interviewed several witnesses and later discovered that the booty had been divided between the two murderers in Bullionville, near Pioche. John A. Johnson had taken his share to gamble in Pioche, NV while Wilson continued on to Idaho with the young woman, Jessie Clevenger.

The sheriff scoured every town between Kanab UT and Pioche NV looking for John Johnson. Approximately, sometime in about the middle of January 1887, Sheriff Mulvenon learned that Johnson was 60 miles from Eureka, UT. Having received a tip, Sheriff Turner of Pioche, informed him where Johnson could be found.

John A. Johnson was working at cutting and hauling wood when he heard the sheriff was looking for him. He then fled to Duckwater, NV where the sheriff tracked him down and found him working on a farm. Sheriff Mulvenon promptly arrested him.

During the arrest, Johnson denied everything – even being in Arizona. He was chained and cuffed and hauled to the nearest jail. After reconsidering, he finally told the sheriff that Wilson had taken the girl and his share of the plunder to Oakley, Idaho. Johnson was completely broke and was working just to earn a meal. He said he'd gambled away his portion of the $500.

Johnson was lodged in the Kanab jail to await the sheriff's return while Mulvenon continued on his manhunt. He still had to find the other outlaw who had taken the girl with him.

He followed the trail of the murderer through Utah and into Idaho, and with help from officers from Pocatello, ID, he finally located Frank Wilson and Jessie Clevenger in Oakley, Idaho in the Shoshone area working for a Charles Lampman. It was reported that he found them dining together before he promptly arrested them. Another account says Frank Wilson was playing a card game when he was arrested.

In Idaho, the sheriff also found the horse team near the place where the fugitives lived. This was the final proof that they were in possession of the wagon that had belonged to Samuel Clevenger. Mulvenon wanted the man who had bought the team from Wilson as a trial witness so he hired him to take the team to Prescott. He promised to reimburse him the money that was paid for the team and to pay his way back home after his testimony and witness.

The old road near the Nevada line through Grouse Creek, in northern UT and into Idaho was a less traveled road in those days, the more popular one being through Snowville, UT and into Idaho. The outlaw would have wanted to take the road less traveled as they hid out. The small settlement of Oakley was a perfect place to stop but they couldn't hide from Sheriff Mulvenon.

The sheriff separated Jessie from Wilson, locking Wilson in jail, and hired a woman to care for Jessie. The sheriff would later include the amount he paid the woman into a reimbursement request presented to the Yavapai County.

Jessie was in the early stage of a pregnancy and Sheriff Mulvenon handled her with great care. When he questioned her about what had happened, she said she dared not tell the truth as her life was at risk. When he assured her she was in no danger, she rested easier but would not talk at that time.

Wilson did the same, claiming he was innocent of any wrongdoing. When confronted with the knowledge that Johnson had told the sheriff where to find his accomplice, Wilson accused Johnson of lying about everything.

On February 5th, on their way to pick up Johnson, Sheriff W.J. Mulvenon and Ms. Jessie Clevenger secured rooms in the Gem Hotel in Nevada for the night while Wilson was accommodated in the local jail. It was not until Wilson and Johnson were both in jail that Sheriff Mulvenon brought the seriousness of the situation to Jessie and she finally told her story of what happened.

The group was brought back to Prescott, where the men were put in the Prescott jailhouse.

The sheriff was interested to verify who had murdered the old couple, why they were murdered and if any money was stolen. There was no money found on any of the arrested parties, their only goods, the clothing on their backs.

Jessie was put into a good home with Mrs. John Hartin, where she remained until it was time for her baby to be born.

She then went into confinement at the hospital. The following photo is the only known photo of Jesse Clevenger.

NOTE: According to an obituary of Mrs. John Hartin, resident of Prescott at the time of these events and who was the mother of 10 children, also had 3 brothers: John Roberts – who later wrote about the murders; Jim Roberts – who later became a deputy sheriff, and according to the written account by John Roberts, befriended Jessie and became a confidant; and Ed Roberts, who was the proprietor of the OK Meat Market in Prescott for many years. – *Weekly Journal Miner*, Prescott, AZ (February 17, 1922)

E10: Jessie Clevenger

4

Jessie's Story

Many were concerned about the fate of the adopted girl, Jessie Clevenger. Her story and testament was well recorded, as she was adamant in her statements. The events as described by her began on the day after old man Clevenger buried his money beside the big rock near the campground. That morning, she was horrified at what happened.

It was reported in the Arizona Weekly that when she answered questions, especially at the trial, that she told a straightforward story and could not be shaken in any cross-examination. She never varied about her version of the story.

After she was ready to confide in the sheriff about what had happened, she told the truth. She was promised safety and protection by Mulvenon.

She told Sheriff Mulvenon that they were all in the camp on the morning of the murders. It was barely dawn, when she approached the fire, preparatory to making coffee, and noticed Johnson standing there. He was in a rage. She watched him bare his arms with an ax in hand and strike Mr. Clevenger on the head with the ax as the old man emerged from the tent. According to an account published in the Arizona Champion, and several other newspapers, Johnson screamed, "You old s-n of a b---h, you have lived long enough!" The old man fell into the campfire and Jessie saw Johnson pull Clevenger out and drag him around the tent.

In sheer terror, Jessie ran off some distance before she heard Mrs. Clevenger scream and call out her name. She turned and started back only to hear the groans of the unfortunate woman who was being murdered in the tent by Wilson with a single blow to the head using an axe.

Jessie began to beg for her life and was told they would spare her, provided she told no one about the murders. If she divulged the secret, her fate would be the same.

The two hired men discovered the money belt containing the $500 hidden inside the tent. After they gathered any items they wanted to keep, they buried the old people in a shallow hole that was dug close to the road. The couple was thrown in the grave, wood was piled on top, along with the mattress and blankets, and a fire started. After the fire had burned down and the bedding was consumed, some dirt was thrown in the hole. Jessie said that Wilson and Johnson divided the money found inside the tent where old man Clevenger slept.

Jessie did not mention the money that was buried under the big rock. For some reason, she chose to keep that a secret. It could have been from habit because she had not told anyone about the money that was secretly buried by her adopted father. She never mentioned it to anyone before, during or after the trial. She was just a young frightened girl who was dealing with a pregnancy that was unexpected and who had been held captive by an outlaw for months.

She continued her story. From there, she said they drove the wagon and team into Kanab, and somewhere along the way, they sold off the herd of horses, pocketing the proceeds. They bought some supplies along with extra bedding before they moved on to the interior of Utah.

They traveled across southern Utah on the long road toward Idaho, dodging towns along the way and traveling into Nevada. Johnson and Wilson parted ways at Bullionville, near Pioche, NV. Wilson and Jessie continued up the trail into Idaho where they rented a small house in Oakley located in the Shoshone area.

Johnson stayed in Nevada where he enjoyed gambling. As a prolific gambler, he kept in touch with Wilson since his share of the money kept dwindling whenever he struck a gambling game. Sometimes when he was broke, he would go live with Wilson and Jessie, working at nearby odd jobs. Other times, he had no trouble finding work at nearby mines and farms in Nevada. Wilson compelled Jessie – under threat of death, to live with him as his wife and she was threatened with death should she ever betray the secret of the murder.

Through all of this, she held her council, never telling either of them about the money that lay buried in the ground back at the camp where the Clevenger's had been murdered. In fact, she never told *anyone* at that time about that hidden cache of currency, silver and gold.

The Trial: Frank Wilson and John A. Johnson

As the story of the horrific murders began to circulate, a man named Barney came forward and stated that he had previously camped with the Clevenger Party in May. He met Wilson, Johnson and the girl, all riding in the wagon, on the same morning of the murders and within eight to fifteen miles of the scene. To ward off suspicion of anything wrong, John A. Johnson told this man, Mr. Barney, that Clevenger had gone out hunting and if he saw him to tell him to hurry up, as it was late and they were compelled to travel on.

The Sheriff continued to search for other eyewitnesses. With the outlaws in jail, the court proceedings would begin.

District Attorney John C. Herndon eventually dropped the charges against the girl in exchange for her testimony against the two men. All parties involved felt that she was an innocent victim of terrible circumstances and should not be held liable for anything that occurred. There was no possible way that she could have escaped and attempted to find help. She was kept isolated and was guarded at all times.

In the beginning, both men said they were innocent, and blamed each other for the crime. At the arraignment in March, Wilson informed the court that he was unable to employ counsel, and the court appointed Col. Eggers for him. Opposing the defendant and representing the territory was District Attorney Herndon, with Judge Wright presiding.

Frank Wilson duly entered a plea of "not guilty". Johnson did the same. It was a while before they knew that Jessie Clevenger had given a statement about what had happened. The trial was scheduled for Monday, March 28, 1887 to be held in the courthouse in Prescott, AZ, but was postponed until June. Even though they were indicted at the April term of court, in filing affidavits of the impossibility of recruiting material witnesses, the trial was postponed until the June term.

Each man was given a separate trial and each testified about the events that happened on the day that the Clevenger's were murdered.

Mr. John A. Johnson was dressed for the occasion in a blue shirt, gray coat and blue overalls, his curly hair carefully oiled and combed down to a mathematical nicety. John Johnson stated that he was innocent and had not even been in the camp when the murders were committed. His statement was long and rambling as he described his actions that day. He claimed that he left the camp early on a horse hunt and much later was overtaken by Wilson and Jessie riding in the wagon. They told him that the old people had gone to Utah by another route. Johnson claimed that he never saw the old folks again that morning after he started on the horse hunt.

After his statement, Jessie Clevenger was called to tell her story. While having a degree of pertness in answering questions, she told an apparently straightforward story and could not be shaken in her cross-examination. She had told the same story before to Sheriff Mulvenon and the grand jury. Her story didn't stray from the facts she previously shared. She stated again that Johnson had killed Samuel Clevenger with an ax and that Frank Wilson had hit Charlotte Clevenger and killed her.

At the Wilson trial, the courthouse was packed with spectators. Frank Wilson who was unshaven, but otherwise presented a respectable appearance, had changed his plea. He pled guilty and claimed that he had acted alone. This was a shock to the whole court. No one expected this to happen and after his plea was introduced, it was his turn to testify and explain his decision to plead guilty.

He was an intelligent and good-looking man, over thirty years of age. While making no marked outward manifestation of emotion, it could readily be seen that beneath his assured expression, he felt keenly aware of the situation.

He was somewhat inclined to nervousness as he now claimed that he was guilty and that he alone had committed the crime. The courtroom was abuzz with surprised reactions as the judge hammered his gavel and demanded silence.

After it was quiet, Frank Wilson explained. He said that Johnson was innocent, that he did nothing wrong, that Wilson alone was responsible. The court was enthralled with this confession, especially after hearing the testimonies of John Johnson and Jessie Clevenger. Once again, the judge had to demand silence in order to continue.

In his testimony, Frank Wilson stated that on the morning of the killings, Johnson was sent out by the old man to hunt up the horses that had strayed during the night. While he was gone, Wilson got into a quarrel with Clevenger about the girl, Jessie. He was tired of the abuse he had witnessed from the old man toward his adopted daughter and so he expressed this to Clevenger. It turned into a fight and he grabbed the axe, swung it and killed the old man.

The room was hushed as the audience listened to the grim account. Wilson kept his eyes forward and never wavered in his confession, even though his voice broke once or twice.

He continued, explaining that Mrs. Clevenger witnessed the killing and he was afraid to let her live, so he killed her also. He claimed that Jessie saw the horrible crimes and he made her assist him while he buried the bodies.

Then the two of them took the wagon and effects and went in search of Johnson. When they found him, Wilson told him that the Clevenger's had met some friends and joined them in their camp to continue their journey by another route.

Wilson, Johnson and Jessie continued to Utah until they reached Toquerville. While there, Wilson traded off some of the horses. He stated that when Johnson asked him "what would Clevenger say", Wilson admitted to him that he had killed them, and threatened that if Johnson told anyone, Wilson would say that he'd helped to kill them both.

The three remained together until they reached Carbondale where they parted company, Wilson taking Jessie with him. Before they separated, Wilson gave him $200 and a team of horses. He again threatened Johnson that if he told, Wilson would blame the crime on him.

In court, he emphasized several times that Johnson was an innocent man.

When Johnson was asked about Wilson's story, Johnson explained that he had begun to feel ill that morning and started on the trail ahead of the Clevenger party. When Wilson and Jessie caught up with him, Johnson couldn't explain why he didn't suspect the absence of Samuel and Charlotte Clevenger, or his lack of curiosity about their disappearance. He also couldn't explain his willingness to accept a share of the plunder.

Jessie Clevenger was the main witness in court. She was expecting a baby soon and still lived in the Hartin household. When it was Jessie's turn to testify, she told the story that she'd told to the sheriff. That Johnson had killed her adopted father and Wilson had killed her adopted mother. Nothing in her testimony deviated from her original story.

Afterward, when Jessie was shown the signed confession by Wilson, she vehemently denied its truth in every way, and repeated again the story as she did on the witness stand. She added, "If you were going to hang me for saying this, then go ahead, because I cannot vary from my testimony."

The confession by Wilson seemed to trump any evidence to the contrary. It didn't matter what other testimonies they had from other people, only Wilson's confession counted.

The trial was short, and the jury wasted little time returning with a verdict of guilty for both men and a death sentence of hanging.

The jury consisted of the following men: C.T. Rodgers, Henry Siddles, Chas. Collins, Geo. Hoxworth, H.C. Lockett, J.S. Sessions, Geo. M. Bogley, G.R. Hopeter, J.B. Elmore, O.A. Ensign, John Reese and W. Williams.

On June 20, 1887, both men were sentenced to hang on Friday, August 12, 1887, although, there was a movement begun with the goal to have John A. Johnson exonerated and his conviction commuted, therefore, saving him from the gallows. It was reported: "Messrs. Eggers Howard, counsel for Johnson, submitted the confession of Wilson to Governor C. Meyer Zulick, who listened to their arguments and interviewed the prisoners." It was up to the governor to issue a reprieve or commutation of the court sentence.

One report by the Arizona Champion Newspaper stated that Wilson frequently said that he did not expect any executive clemency and did not want it. He said that living had been a hell to him for some time and he wanted to have done with it.

The Weekly Citizen newspaper had a short interview with Wilson during the trial period. He told them that his name, Wilson, was an assumed name, not his real name and that he was from Michigan. He refused to divulge more information, stating that if his real identity became known, and his relatives informed, then they would learn of the disgrace he had brought to them.

On the evening after the day in court when Wilson had confessed to the murders, he requested another interview, stating that the alleged confession published was not a correct one and he volunteered to write another one. When the newspaper later tried to pick it up, he had changed his mind. One report from the Prescott Courier stated that Wilson wanted them to change their account of his confession. He indignantly wrote to them:

"Ed. Courier – Dear Sir, In your paper of 10th instant there is an article headed "Wilson's confession." I did make a statement in which I admitted that I killed Clevenger and his wife and that I alone am responsible for the crime of which Johnson and myself are convicted, but I never said that Jessie Clevenger helped me to bury the bodies of Clevenger and his wife. I never even mentioned her name in my statement. If you will correct that mistake, you will greatly oblige a murderer. Frank Willson."

It is interesting to note that in this specific document Wilson spelled his name with two L's. Reasoning for this might have been related to his statement about using a false identity so as to not shame his family name. It may have been a last minute attempt to avoid having his last name associated with the murder by convincing the people at that time to use the name "Willson" instead of "Wilson".

There was a rumor that the two men planned a ruse, whereby one of the convicted men would serve life imprisonment, if the other confessed to the murders. It was said that while awaiting a definite execution, they agreed to draw straws, the loser to assume all blame for the killings and save the other's neck, who, if pardoned, was to return to Prescott and kill Jessie Clevenger for testifying against them. As the story goes, Wilson drew the long straw and made the confession that he alone killed the Clevenger's.

Another story likens the ruse to a card game, where Wilson drew the wrong card, was the loser and assumed the role as the sole killer.

The hanging was set for August 12, 1887. On that day, both men prepared for the execution. They rose early, took a bath and had their hair trimmed and cut. They were both shaved by W. F. Landgrebe; Johnson preferred to keep his mustache and Wilson liked a bit of a beard. Then they dressed in clean clothes.

At 6:30 AM, Jessie Clevenger called at the jail for an interview with Wilson. Her baby would be born on August 30th, so she was very large with a child. It took place in the jailer's room in the presence of Sheriff Mulvenon.

Wilson wanted to kiss her, but she waved him away and accused him of lying in his confession. At previous interviews, the girl had been patient and submissive to Wilson, assenting to everything he said. This morning, however, she displayed more nerve, charging that Wilson, by his so-called confession, had injured her. Referring to this statement, she remarked, *"You know you lied, Wilson! You know that Johnson killed the old man with that –"*(pointing to the instrument with which the old man was killed, which was standing in the jailer's room), *"and that afterwards you drew it through the fire to take the blood off it! You know that Johnson's clothes were splattered with blood and that you and he burned them up!"* She was in tears at this point, her passionate pleas pathetic.

During this conversation, Wilson hung his head and made no reply. When she finished, he simply walked away to the jail cell without bidding her good-bye. Jessie was crushed.

The officers and many people who had convened with both of the condemned men were skeptical concerning the truth of his confession, and were convinced that Wilson had lied. Even as the governor entertained the requests for clemency toward Johnson, there was an uncertain feeling.

The confession was contrary to Jessie's testimony and statements made by other witnesses about Johnson. Nevertheless, the sentence had been stipulated and only Johnson had a chance of avoiding the noose.

Wilson and Johnson, dressed in new suits of clothing ordered from J.W. Wilson had their picture taken by Erwin Baer, the photographer. At 11:15, just as Wilson had lighted a fresh cigar, remarking at the same time that he did not "propose to lose any time", Sheriff Mulvenon, Under-Sheriff

Waddell, Governor C. Meyer Zulick, Secretary Bayard, Rev. J. C. Houghton and Sam C. Miller entered the jail. The death warrants were read to the prisoners by the Under-Sheriff. Wilson remained unmoved, but Johnson was visibly affected.

During the interim between this and 12 o'clock, when the sheriff arrived for the prisoners, Johnson remained in a cell with Catholic priest Father Franciscus X. Gubitosi, while Wilson smoked and chatted in the corridor with his watchers and the few visitors present. Other members of the clergy, including protestant ministers W. L. Allbright, and Reverent C.C. Wright, called at the jail, but Wilson, professing no belief in God, refused to see them. Another visitor, Mrs. Bishop from the Holiness Mission also called.

As the clock struck 12, Sheriff Mulvenon, Governor Zulick and Secretary Bayard again entered the jail. Wilson was asked if he had anything to say. He replied that he had, but only reiterated his former statement, exonerating both Johnson and Jessie Clevenger from any participation in the crime.

When John Johnson was asked for a statement, he said that he had nothing to say except that he was innocent of the charge. At this point, Governor Zulick handed a document to Sheriff Mulvenon which he read and informed Johnson that it was a reprieve for him until September 23. He was overcome with joy and warmly grasped Sheriff Mulvenon by the hand, then shook hands with Wilson and said, "Good-bye and God bless you." He then broke completely down and retired to one corner of the corridor where he wept and sobbed like a child.

Another account describes a more dramatic scene. Governor Zulick was suspicious of the confession made by Wilson and meant to put both men on the scaffold together and test them out in the presence of death. He fancied that one or both would break down at the last minute and tell the truth.

The scaffolding held two traps, two ropes, with everything ready for a double execution. Governor Zulick stood at a window on the second floor of the courthouse overlooking the yard. He told Mulvenon that if he waved his handkerchief out of the window at the last minute it meant a reprieve for the man named Johnson. The governor had a good view of the gallows from that second floor window.

The sun was shining hot on this day. Few people chose to be out in its glare. Those who were invited to the hanging stood silently, enduring the heat with fortitude.

Wilson came out first and walked toward the yard, and then Johnson followed him, supported by a deputy sheriff on both sides, as he could not walk. As he paused, Zulick's handkerchief waved from the window and Johnson was a reprieved man until September 23, when another decision for his fate would be made.

Frank Wilson was then taken out to the jail yard, a little brick-walled courtyard on the east side of the old county courthouse, and was led up the stairs of the scaffold. He glanced at the blue sky, as wispy clouds hung suspended above. For a moment, he may have seen the future that would never be. He ascended each step with a firm and unfaltering stride, displaying remarkable nerve. He was again asked if he had anything to say, when he stepped forward and repeated his remarks previously stated in the jail.

With a nod to several men that he knew in the crowd, he said good-bye and retreated to the back of the scaffold. He took off his slippers and took his position on the death trap. While Sheriff Mulvenon pinioned his legs, deputy Burton and Hickey pinioned his arms. The black cap was drawn over his head while a smile still played upon his lips. Deputy Tacket adjusted the fatal noose when Sheriff Mulvenon sprang the trap at precisely 12 minutes after the noon hour. The body of Frank Wilson hung suspended by the neck. Only two almost imperceptible movements of the body were visible after the trap fell.

Dr. Robinson timed the pulse for eighteen and a half minutes, when he declared life extinct and the rope was cut. During those eighteen minutes, the crowd stood mute, respect for the dead evident in their manner. Men died in all manner of ways and sometimes it was difficult to understand this type of death. It was even more puzzling when it was suffered with dignity and great bravery by the condemned.

It was determined at that time that his neck had broken from the fall and he had not suffered. The body was then lowered into the waiting coffin and given to undertaker Randal, where it was taken to Citizens Cemetery for burial. His grave is not listed in the records, but it wasn't unusual for some to become unknown graves.

It was not a public execution, but there were several representatives from newspapers there: Journal – Miner, Hoof and Horn and Courier – Prescott; Chronicle, Post and Call – San Francisco; Arizonian – Phoenix; Champion – Flagstaff, Democrat – Albuquerque; Globe-Democrat – St. Louis; Citizen – Tucson.

Between 1875 and 1903, there were eleven legal hangings in Yavapai County. Frank Wilson was number six. I've included a list of all of them for your scrutiny. These hangings took place over a period of 28 years, and was punishment reserved for only the most severe crimes.

Hangings in Prescott, Yavapai County, Arizona Territory (1885-1903)

1875 – August 6, First legal hanging in Yavapai County. Manuel Abiles (or Aviles) 27-30 years old, was accused, tried, and convicted of the killing of a ranch hand, Gregorio Eredia, in the Verde Settlement in April 1875. Ed Bowers, county sheriff, presided. Evidence was circumstantial, and it was discovered, decades later, that it was a neighbor who had killed the ranch hand in a dispute over water rights.

1878 – March 31, James Malone hanged on a scaffold in the Prescott jail yard for the murder of Private Richard L. Lawler at Camp Mohave. Sheriff Bowers presided.

1881 – February 10. Henry H. Hall executed in the jail yard in Prescott for the murder of saloon owner H. J. Bishop in Flagstaff. Sheriff John Walker presided.

1882 – February 3. John Berry hanged in the jailhouse courtyard for the murder of Michael Shores at Tiptop on March 1881 – Sheriff John Walker presided

1886 – February 5. Dennis W. Dilda executed in the Prescott courthouse yard for killing Jim Jenkins, a prospector. Sentence carried out by Sheriff William J. Mulvenon.

1887 – August 12. Frank Wilson hanged in the gallows yard of the Prescott Courthouse Plaza for the murders of Samuel and Charlotte Clevenger near Kanab, Utah, in January 1887

1888 – March 2. Martin Duran executed in Prescott for the murder of his estranged common-law wife, Reyes Baca in Flagstaff on September 18, 1887. Sheriff Mulvenon presided.

1898 – June 3. Fleming Parker hanged for the killing of Lee Norris, Assistant County Attorney when Parker was awaiting trial for train robbery. Sheriff G.C. Ruffner presided

1903 – July 31 Execution of Eligio (Hilario?) Hidalgo and Francisco Rentezia, for killing Charles Goddard and Frank Cox at Goddard Station on February 1, 1903. Sheriff Roberts presided.

Information taken from the Hangings Vertical File and from Parker Anderson's book, Wicked Prescott (2016)

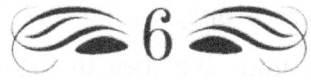

After the Hanging

When questioned during the trial about the valuables stolen from Mr. and Mrs. Clevenger, the guilty parties claimed the only money taken from old man Clevenger was what he had carried with him, and the profit received from the sale of the herd of horses. There was no mention of the other money, the proceeds from the sale of the property in Fort Thomas.

It was supposed that there was more money at stake, but there was no way to prove it. Everyone knew the Clevenger's had sold their place for a substantial sum, but no one knew what they had done with the money. It was speculated that there could have been more money involved and the murderers could have taken it.

Only Jessie knew the truth about the money. It was a long time before she confided in anyone about the buried cache of currency, silver and gold. After all that she suffered, witnessing the murders, running and hiding with outlaws under threat of death for months, must have put a fear deep into her heart and distanced her from other people. I imagine she was afraid to trust anyone.

She had remained with Mrs. Hartin for more than two years. Her baby daughter had been adopted when she was 18 months old by Mr. and Mrs. Jim Vanderburg, a merchant in Stanton, AZ. She was a bright child and was the joy of the Vanderburg's home, until she died at the age of three years old.

E11: Jim Roberts

Included in a testament written by John Roberts, there is a short notation about his brother Jim Roberts, also the brother of Mrs. Hartin. Even though his name was left out of the testament, research has put a name to him from the clues in the story. It states that he became well acquainted with Jessie Clevenger. Being a reliable man, and one of the few people that she considered a friend, Jessie trusted him and discussed details of the murder with him. She waited a long time, until the beginning of the year of 1889, two years after her rescue, before entrusting him with her secret.

She told him about the money and how her adopted father had buried it in the ground and she contended that it was still there. She was certain that the murderers did not find the money.

On January 1, 1889, Jim was appointed deputy sheriff and deputy assessor by Bucky O'Neill, who had taken over the sheriff's office of Yavapai County, having been elected that fall. The following April, Bucky sent him on a trip to the northern part of the country. The object of the trip was to subpoena witnesses for a case going before the grand jury.

Jessie Clevenger urged him to go to the spot where the money was buried and get it. She described the big rock by the side of the road where old man Clevenger said he had buried the money on the night before he was murdered.

Leaving Prescott, Jim started on his journey. He planned to do what Jessie had asked. She insisted on secrecy, so he honored her request and did not tell anyone his plans, not even his superior, Bucky O'Neill.

On April 29, 1889, Jim Roberts stopped at House Rock Valley and just happened to fall in with Harry Clayton, who carried the mail from Johnson, Utah to Lee's Ferry. If you recall, he was one of the people who reportedly found the graves of the Clevenger's up on Buckskin Mountain.

They rode together to Johnson, and along the way, he kept a sharp lookout for the place described by Jessie as the place where the murders had been committed. It was reputed to be about five miles from the Utah border.

Assuming that the mail carrier would know about events, Jim brought up the subject of the murders. Without mentioning any specific interest, Jim was able to casually draw the story from Clayton. The mail carrier told Jim all about it and even pointed out the exact spot. The men could see that some of the charred bed clothing was still there, near several big rocks in the area, one in particular where Jim assumed the money had probably been buried. Glancing at it while he passed, the ground around it looked as if it had been disturbed and something could have been dug up.

Assuming he was looking at the right rock and assuming he could judge "at a glance", since he never stepped off his horse to examine the ground when he was with Clayton, he rode on with his conclusions. He wanted to keep Jessie's confidence and didn't want Clayton to suspect him of snooping.

When Jim returned home, he told Jessie someone had already dug it up and suggested that the murderers probably got it. She was adamant that they did not take it, having lived with Wilson and knowing he didn't have a great deal of cash. She confided once again what her stepfather had said when he'd buried the money.

The following month after Jim's trip, May 3rd 1889, Jessie married Joseph Spear and they went to Colorado. It was during this time that Jessie received confirmation that a previously requested homesteading deed that her father Samuel had applied for near Durango Colorado was granted. This deed extended the ownership of a 160 acre parcel of land homesteaded in Colorado to Samuel Clevenger and his heirs. This would have given Jessie reason to travel to Colorado to claim this land as her own.

John A. Johnson, who had his death sentence commuted until September 23rd, 1886, was sentenced to life in prison, where he was registered as prisoner 499 at the territorial prison near Yuma.

He assumed his previous indifference as he tried to assure himself that his respite would eventually result in a pardon of sentence. He had promised forthcoming evidence to corroborate the statements made by Wilson, and had yet to fulfill his word, which greatly angered the Governor.

It was uncertain if Governor Zulick would further interfere in the matter, but after Johnson had served six years in prison, he was pardoned by the governor. One statement in a newspaper implied that Governor C. Meyer Zulick had an issue with his conscience concerning the confession of Frank Wilson, and had wondered if it was true, since many believed it wasn't. Governor Zulick didn't want to set a killer free, but in the end, he pardoned John Johnson.

It isn't known if Johnson provided further evidence as promised. After his release, John A. Johnson lived and died while living in Phoenix for several years after his pardon.

Postscript for trial

Confession: The Arizona Weekly Citizen published an account of the confession made by Frank Wilson for the crime:

"The following is a correct copy of Wilson's statement, the one heretofore published being incorrect in many particulars. Prescott, August 9th 1887".

"This is to certify that John A. Johnson is innocent of the crime of which he stands convicted on the 20th day of May, 1886, the day on which Samuel Clevenger was killed. Johnson

left the camp early in the morning to hunt up some horses that had strayed during the night, with orders to drive them on to water as soon as he found them, as there was no water where we were camped. After Johnson had been gone from camp about one hour, I, Frank Wilson, became engaged in a quarrel with Samuel Clevenger and his wife, Charlotte Clevenger, and killed them both in the same spot where their bodies were found. Then I took the wagon and the rest of the stock and overtook Johnson on the road with the rest of the horses. I told Johnson that Clevenger and his wife had gone to Utah by another road with some friends that caught up with us that morning, as there was a road that turned off, that went into Utah. He believed me until we got to Tokeville, where I traded off some of the horses, and then Johnson asked me what Clevenger would say if he knew I was trading off his horses. I told Johnson that I had killed them, and he had better keep still about it for I would say that he helped to kill them both and I made Johnson take some of the horses and some money, so he would not say anything about it. I am ready to meet my fate, but I do not want to see an innocent man hang for my crime. (Signed) Frank Willson"

Sentencing: The sentencing of Frank Wilson was published in the Arizona Weekly Journal-Miner and was read by Judge Wright in clear and impressive tones:

"You, Frank Wilson, were indicted at the adjourned November term of this Court, begun and held in this

courthouse in the month of March, 1887, by the grand jury of Yavapai county, Arizona Territory, for the crime of killing and murdering Samuel Clevenger on the 21st day of May, 1886, on the Buckskin Mountains in said County and Territory. At your arraignment upon the indictment, you informed the Court that you were unable to employ counsel; thereupon, the Court proceeded to appoint for you able and experienced counsel, to the end that all your constitutional and legal rights might be fully protected; thereupon, your arraignment upon that indictment was made; to which arraignment, after the usual statutory time, you duly entered your plea of "not guilty". Thereby putting yourself upon the country. And the cause was then, upon your application, and in order that you might have every reasonable opportunity to make good your defense, continued to the present term of this court. And at the present term of this court, the country – that is to say, a jury of twelve good and lawful men, on the 20th day of June, 1887, duly convicted you of the crime of murder of the first degree – the said jury to their verdict affixing the death penalty declaring that you shall suffer death for such crime, notwithstanding your counsel, at every stage of your trial and defense, have defended you with commendable fidelity and marked ability. It now becomes my painful duty to give

legal effect to that verdict, by pronouncing judgment thereon.

Have you now any legal cause to show why the judgment of the Court, upon that conviction and verdict, should not at this time be pronounced and entered against you?"

Wilson – *"No, Sir."*

"No legal cause being shown by you why judgment should not now be pronounced, it is by the Court ordered and adjudged that you, Frank Wilson, are guilty of the crime of murder of the first degree; and the order, judgment and sentence of the Court in your case is that you be punished therefor, as follows: that you be taken hence by the Sheriff of the county of Yavapai Territory of Arizona, aforesaid, to your place of confinement and there securely kept until Friday, the 12th day of August, 1887, and on that day, that you be taken by said Sheriff from your place of confinement, between the hours of ten o'clock in the forenoon and two o'clock in the afternoon of the said 12th day of August, 1887, to such place in the said county of Yavapai, as may be selected by the said Sheriff of said County, and that you be then and there, at such place, by the said Sheriff, hanged by the neck until you be dead, dead, dead, and may the Lord have mercy on you!"

The Treasure Map

$2,000-$6,000 in money in 1886 could well be worth hundreds of thousands of dollars and possibly as high as a million dollars today. Silver Certificates can sell at auction between $15,000 and $20,000 each. According to the Bureau of Labor Statistics consumer price index, when comparing the Silver Certificates with the modern dollar, the dollar experienced an average inflation rate of 2.49% per year. Prices in 2017 were 2392.0% higher than prices in 1886. In other words, $100 in the year 1886 is equivalent in purchasing power to $2,492.02 in 2017, a difference of $2,392.02 over 131 years. The inflation rate in 2017 was 1.99%.

E12: 1886 Silver and Gold Coin

E13: 1886 Silver Certificate $1

Old gold and silver coins sell for much more than their worth in metal. An 1886 Gold Liberty Eagle in proof condition recently sold for $88,125.00, whereas an 1886 Gold Liberty Head Double sold for $228,000! An 1886 Morgan Silver dollar sold for $8,812.50. Even small change is valuable, as an 1886 Liberty nickel sold for $2,415.00!

This stash of wealth could still be out there. There could be a fortune somewhere along the trail between House Rock Valley and Kanab.

Tracking the money has been an interesting journey. It is important to examine all of the facts – as if following a trail marked on a map – that leads to the treasure! What is really the truth and what are the lies? We need to examine all the possibilities and rule out the ridiculous. The discovery of the hidden money back in 1886 would have been newsworthy and yet not a word is ever said about it.

There is still a lot of missing information about Clevenger's full story, some facts that seem to be at variance with others, and a sense of secretive maneuvering on the part of some of the involved parties. What is really the truth and what are the lies?

There are dozens of possibilities about the fate of the money buried in the desert. Did the outlaws take it? Did Jessie return after her marriage and find it herself? Did any of the sheriff's deputies dig it up and keep it? I wouldn't imagine them doing so as they were honest and upstanding citizens sworn to uphold the law.

Did the postman, while traveling back and forth, discover it buried beside the big rock? Did John A. Johnson see Mr. Clevenger burying it that night, and after all was quiet, did he dig it up and keep it all to himself; maybe hiding it somewhere nearby or along the trail?

How many other people, while poking and prodding around the camp area, might have discovered it?

All of the above are possibilities that are conceivable, but that much money would have been a bonanza hard to hide in those days. If someone found it, they would have suddenly become rich and surely, the neighbors would have noticed; the newspapers would have reported it; someone would have certainly received a substantial reward for turning it in. But there was no mention of a discovery or any indication that anyone accrued extra wealth. In fact, before the outlaws were caught, Wilson and Johnson were always working odd jobs to get by. Johnson would sometimes move back in with Wilson when he would be out of work or low on income.

The many other people mentioned in this book all lived lives that were not indicative of someone who discovered such wealth in 1886.

Is it possible that the treasure, known only to Jessie Clevenger, could still be buried and hidden in the Arizona desert, somewhere in the Buckskin Mountains, waiting for the right person to come and claim it.?

No one suspected that there was a buried treasure in the campsite. It was known only as the site where a terrible murder had been committed. Everyone assumed that the outlaws had taken anything of value with them. Even after they were discovered, and arrested, they admitted to taking the $500 and selling the horses. Why would they keep any other stolen money a secret? They freely admitted what they did wrong so why not tell about the other money?

The distance between Prescott and the House Rock Valley area is approximately 290 miles. For a young girl who had just given birth to a baby right after the hanging, it would have been difficult to return by herself to retrieve the stash. She had been traumatized by the events of the murder, the abduction afterwards, the threats against her life, and was not likely to be very trusting of others.

It took a few years before she was able to confide in Jim Roberts, the brother of Mrs. Hartin, the woman who had kindly sheltered her at such a shattered time in her young life.

The desert along the Utah/Arizona border hides many secrets. The Clevenger treasure was hidden somewhere in the Buckskin Mountains, near the House Rock Area. These are all marked clearly on maps. The trail that the postman rode between Kanab, Johnson and Lee's Ferry should be easy to locate. If the Clevenger's camp area was right along the road, it should be simple to find.

Finding the gold could be as easy as locating a trail that a wagon could go down. The challenge is that new maps no longer include all the little trails that were once used. A horse with a lone rider could ride anywhere, whereas a group of wagons, herding cows or horses, would have to use another path, near water and feed, cleared of impediments. People with guides tried new paths that suited them and opened a new trail. When automobiles were invented, new roads were developed by modern machinery that suited the transport and the old ones were forgotten or paved over.

Arizona is a state that is rich in history. Artifacts belonging to the Native Americans are sacred to their ancestry. Hunting for these items is against the law in Arizona for fortune seekers. Looking for treasure on State and Federal Land is also forbidden. An Archeologist with all the proper paperwork can be permitted to excavate in those areas with the correct permission.

Looking for answers about the mystery of Clevenger's missing money should be done correctly. Be sure to learn about the Arizona treasure hunting laws before you search.

Looking for Gold

With that in mind, I was invited to accompany Historical Advisor and Archaeologist Stephen B. Shaffer, and a small team of treasure hunters, to explore the old trails that twisted through the Buckskin Mountains. Stephen is the author of Utah's Hidden Treasures, Out of the Dust, Treasures of the Ancients, as well as various other books. He was also featured on National Geographic's Secret History of Gold and the television series America Unearthed.

Our party consisted of Lee Hall and Glen Cottom, local treasure hunters in Southern Utah, along with Internet Researcher David Werner and Photographer Brittney Hess.

The goal was simple, to locate the campsite of the Clevenger family. It is important to note that I have not withheld any information regarding the lost treasure and freely share all that I have learned.

There are a few clues I would like to share that helped us on our journey that could help to lead you to riches. For example, when Frank Wilson gave his testimony, he mentioned a couple of very interesting facts. He said that the campsite was not located near water. He also said there was a road that branched off to head to St. George. It was also recorded that the brutal killing of the Clevenger's took place 5 miles south of the Utah border. You remember that Jessie mentioned that the money was buried near a large rock on the right side of the road (heading north). These are all location clues to help in a search.

Pictured left to right:
E14: Lee Hall, Aaron Werner, Stephen B. Shaffer,
Glenn Cottom

While researching this book, I discovered many clues that may lead on a path to the lost gold, coins and currency. My goal in sharing this information was to inspire someone, or hopefully many, to get into the outdoors, explore the beautiful landscape of Northern Arizona and Southern Utah and learn more about the amazing history of these states. As explorers, we should always respect our landscape, tread only where allowed, and leave the beautiful outdoors just as we found it.

As a writer, I will take the liberty to deviate a little from the facts that were so well presented in this book and explore some of the "what if's" that flowed through my mind. The idea behind this is to allow all the possibilities to be presented so that you can draw your own conclusion as to the ending of this story...for it has not ended. There could still be more information that is not disclosed to the public to answer some of these questions.

- Why did Frank Wilson disclose to the newspaper that he had an assumed name? He signed his confession with two L's. When looking back as early as 1884 and the Graham County indictment his name was spelled with only one L. Was this his attempt to convince the people at the time that his name was Willson (with two L's) to avoid his family learning about the murders and hanging or is it possible he had a completely different name?

- Why did Wilson avoid the more populated areas as he traveled northward with the Clevenger's? What was he hiding from? Did he still owe a debt to the military for the stolen horse and or was he planning one of the most horrific crimes in Arizona Territory?

- Did John A. Johnson know something about Wilson's hidden past? After all, they had known each other previously before meeting again. Could he have threatened to disclose Wilson's true identity if he did not admit to the crime?

- Why did Johnson cut a deal with the governor and promise to disclose more information? What was that information? It was reported that Governor Zulick felt burned by anger over his sparing John A. Johnson's life after Johnson reneged on their deal

- Why did so many people try to protect John A Johnson? If you think about it, Wilson took the blame for the murders, in Prescott, a large number of people signed the petition to save him, the Governor was angry over his reprieve but still released him and 6 years later he allowed him out of prison. Is there more to his story?

- Where did Wilson go wrong? One report by the Arizona Champion Newspaper stated that Wilson frequently said he did not expect any executive clemency and did not want it. He said that living had been a hell to him for some time and he wanted to be done with it. The legal issues with the United States Military, the possible money he owed Clevenger, the murders, the guilt, the relationship with Jessie, knowing what he did to her parents. Was it the stealing of the horse that set these things in motion; one decision that created a snowball effect?

- Where is the missing deed to the Clevenger property? As of the time of the writing of this book, the only deed we were able to locate is the deed to the water and ditch rights. Is there even a deed to the property or did he homestead the land and do a handshake deal with Jerome B. Collins at the time of the sale?

- Was Jerome B. Collins' murder related to Clevenger's? Jerome was murdered in August of the same year as the Clevenger's. Was it possible that Clevenger and Jerome were in deep together and Clevenger decided to high tail it out of town for other reasons?

- When Jessie got married, did she take her honeymoon to the famous Honeymoon Trail that runs near the campsite and claim her rightful inheritance?

I hope that someday these questions will be answered. My honest opinion about the honor of the local citizens involved in every aspect of this incident is nobler then it may seem. You need to remember that there was an orphan girl named Jessie Clevenger who had witnessed a horrendous murder, not just of anyone, but the murder of her legal parents. She was then abducted, abused and left with a child. I believe that there is a high probability that anyone who might have found the money at that time would return it to her or at least a portion of it.

She was a victim of terrible circumstances, not responsible in any way for what occurred. Who would have been so merciless as to keep the money from her?

I don't think anyone found the money. I believe it is still there.

In our quest, as we ventured into the desert, we explored as near to the location as we could ascertain. Not having that "X" to mark the spot on our own map, we had to create a map, scope out a trail and pursue that route. Archeologist Stephen B. Shaffer, with his years of treasure hunting experience, as an avid explorer, helped us isolate our route. Let me tell you a bit about our adventure.

We gathered together equipment that would be helpful in exploring the desert. The most important piece was a Military Grade Prototype Long Range Gold Detector. The one we used could not be purchased in a store but was built specifically for long-range gold hunting. The Long Range detector had to be programmed from a laptop computer with certain frequencies contributed to gold, silver and other metals.

Using old maps and new maps, we spent some time locating the Old Arizona Highway and the Honeymoon Trail. Then working backwards, we located the Navajo Well. We chose to start here because it was reported that this was going to be the next stop for the Clevenger family on their journey northward. Using this area as the starting point, we mapped a course into the Buckskin Mountains, with our group gathering at Pioneer Gap, situated next to Navajo Well just a short distance south of Hwy 89.

We encountered a local sheriff who was investigating a dead body buried in the ground near the Navajo Well. The officer said the grave could have been from an early Native American and stated that there were many graves in that area.

That region also contained pottery shards scattered across the ground and Indian ruins. These are the precious things that should be left alone and untouched by visitors.

On our map, we located a potential target point in the Buckskin Mountains that was not located on State or Federal land and set out to explore. Our trip was carefully planned to happen in the early spring. We avoided the extreme heat of the summer desert by choosing that date. The winds were cool, the sky a faded blue and many of the hedgehog cactuses were blooming, their bright pink flowers dressing up the sandy ground.

We followed the Old Arizona Highway into the Buckskin Mountains, sometimes taking side trails that were hardly used anymore. The terrain was scrubland, with some grassy flats. In the distance, we could see shadowy canyon walls that were faded into the horizon. At one point, when we thought we were in the approximate region (but discovered later that we weren't!) we located an area that was providing a good reading for gold in the ground.

The area was desolate, near some scrub and natural bush shelter with a watering pond for cattle and horses. It looked like it may have been a campsite at one time. We set up shop and started working the area.

We ran the long-range metal detector using a method where you triangulate the gold. We used multiple reference points in the process and narrowed down the search area with each sweep. We were able to isolate the location to about a 3-5 foot area. The equipment told us the target could be 6 feet underground. Without the proper equipment to dig such a spot, we marked it on our map for a return trip. We didn't feel this was the place for the Clevenger gold, but it could have possibly been a gravesite and the gold attached to a tooth; or it could have been another treasure buried at another time.

Not wanting to disturb a possible gravesite without further investigation, we continued to scout out the surrounding area. There were many potential spots but we only had a few hours to search. We passed several campsites and knew we needed more time to check them all. I only wish I could devote more time to this activity! There is a lot of ground to cover in order to locate one baking soda can of money.

We went home empty handed but gained an incredible appreciation for those people that traveled these old roads back in 1886. Some were so rough that even our modern day 4x4's had a challenging time getting around the terrain.

When we started our journey that first day we noticed a memorial plaque located in the Navajo Well/Honeymoon Trail area. The well was a natural spring which supplied water to travelers, their horses and oxen. It was a favorite stopping place for those weary and thirsty trekkers from 1877 to 1927, especially the bridal parties going to and from the St. George Mormon temple. The well was also the next stop on the Clevenger's journey. There are no more travelers who stop there now for water, but in its heyday, it was a beloved oasis for all.

The Honeymoon trail from Navajo Well enters Kanab then proceeds to Pipe Spring, the Rock Canyon Dugway, down Hurricane Cliffs, through Fort Pearce, and then on to St. George and the Toquerville area.

Going in the other direction, toward Arizona, the famous trail crosses the Buckskin Mountains to the House Rock area. Originally created by the Paiute Native Americans, it was used by two Spanish priests in 1776 when they traveled along the base of the Kaibab Plateau. In the 1880s, Arizona historian Will Barnes (the same Will Barnes who witnessed the hanging of Frank Wilson) lived on the Little Colorado River. He enjoyed visiting with the people going past his ranch, to and from St. George, Utah, on their way to be married in the Mormon temple in St George.

In 1934, he wrote an article for Arizona Highways Magazine, and referred to the system of wagon roads as the "Honeymoon Trail." The name stuck, and everyone, including the Mormon Church members themselves, began to refer to this network of trails as such.

The trail was first used in 1881 when a bridal party traveled from Arizona on their way north to St. George, UT to be married in the Mormon Temple. It took twenty days to reach the destination in a wagon with a team of mules or horses. After the trail was blazed, it became a popular route for wedding parties.

One of the greatest challenges was the need to cross the Colorado River. Earlier in 1870, Mormon Church leaders had sent a party of men to establish a fort at present-day Lee's Ferry. By the following year, a regular ferry was operating across the Colorado. In 1872, John D. Lee became the manager of the ferry service. At that time, the charge to cross the river was $1 per wagon and 25¢ per head of cattle.

Just getting down to the river was a challenge. Wagons had to inch down a steep, difficult hill popularly called Lee's Backbone.

After crossing the Colorado River, the journey continued along the Vermilion Cliffs. The trip from there to House Rock covered some extremely dry country. Fortunately, there were springs scattered about a day's travel apart.

From House Rock, the climb to Buckskin Mountains eventually ended at Jacob's Lake. From there, the road turned north to Kanab, just across the Utah border.

Sometimes it's hard to believe that only a hundred-fifty years ago, traveling was so time consuming and took much preparation and sacrifice. We are so accustomed to jumping in our cars, flying in our airplanes – even watching astronauts travel into space.

Our ancestors had great fortitude and strong characters to stay diligent in building our country. The old stories of their challenges are sometimes astonishing and their clever, committed and dogged determination to succeed was the driving force of progress leading us to where we are today.

The Journey

In studying a map of travel routes that were used in 1886, I imagined the Clevenger's and their party reaching Lee's Ferry and making the hazardous crossing with a herd of horses. The weather was calm on the day they crossed (according to historical records), so maybe the water was also gentle.

It was after they achieved that difficult part of the journey and when they had traveled closer to the Utah border that the murders had been committed. I wondered why they waited until then. I imagine that not a lot of people traveled such a difficult trail very often and it must have been a more isolated part of their journey. Was this a murder of passion – as claimed by Frank Wilson – over the callous treatment of the girl, Jessie, or was it for greed, as Jessie implied in her testimony? Could this have been a murder for revenge – the proud soldier Johnson who might have resented being treated similar to a servant?

Would there have been another purpose for traveling with the old couple until almost out of Arizona, before they were dispensed with, and the outlaws could travel more freely into Utah and Idaho?

I also wondered why they buried the bodies so close to the road, that it could be seen by any passerby. I can only surmise that they were in a hurry to move out and get away. If they had been more careful where they disposed of the bodies, it might have been years before they were discovered.

I deduced that both men were somewhat educated. Frank Wilson was able to write a confession while he was in jail, along with an educated letter to the editor of the Prescott Courier, and John A. Johnson had served in the 10th Cavalry where he would have had an opportunity to learn to read and write. He was a gambler, so probably proficient in math.

The 10th Cavalry was composed of stalwart blacks in Army Blue and were nicknamed Buffalo Soldiers by the Arizona Indians. The newspapers described the troopers of the 10th Cavalry as "well behaved and as soldierly-looking set of men that have ever been stationed at Whipple." In 1886, few residents of Arizona Territory – as was the case with most nineteenth century Americans – knew little about the valuable service performed by these soldiers. When Johnson left the Cavalry, he was immediately employed by Samuel Clevenger.

Wilson and Johnson's pursuit and capture, during a time when communication was limited to an occasional telegraph station located in a larger settlement, was a remarkable feat. By avoiding the more populated areas, they were out of reach. When I read about the dedicated lawmen who rode horses for hundreds of miles, in all kinds of weather, far from home and loved ones, I couldn't help but admire their stamina and determination.

For instance, Sheriff William "Billy" Mulvenon had a remarkable record of service. The capture of the murderers of the Clevenger family in the Buckskin range of mountains near Utah proved his fortitude in solving a case with few clues. His persistence during the investigation is regarded as one of the finest pieces of criminal work ever performed in the Southwest during those difficult times.

During his tenure of office, the bloody Tonto Basin vendetta was raging, in which human lives were wantonly sacrificed. Entering the field on horseback with a posse of five of his deputies, he brought that frightful era to a climax by using force and at the cost of a life. But it ended any further violence that throttled immigration and discredited investment by home seekers.

He was born in Belcertown, Mass in October 1850. His family moved to Leavenworth, Kansas in 1857. By 1868, Billy was a government contractor at Fort Harker, when that military post was on the outskirts of Indian depredations and a lawless element of white men. His environment was a border life, but it fitted him in later years of his life in building up society and upholding the law.

Mulvenon worked as a miner and stable-keeper before becoming a sheriff's deputy. Arriving in Prescott in the spring of 1878, after traveling over the Santa Fe Trail on horseback from Fort Leavenworth, Kansas, Mulvenon took up mining and located at the Peck camp in the Bradshaw's. He made investments in that field, with varying success.

Serving four years under Sheriffs Walker and Hinkle, he was nominated by his party for this office and was elected as Yavapai County Sheriff on January 1, 1885. After serving four distinguished years, he retired on January 1, 1889 and was honored as one of Arizona's most efficient sheriffs.

Soon after he retired, he married Ella Johnson, a native of Oregon. He began mining in an area called Turkey Creek in central Arizona and in the early 1890's, sold ice for Jake Mark's wholesale liquor company.

He established the Prescott Crystal Ice Works and was a primary stockholder in the Arizona Brewing Company. He also served as a legislator for two terms in Yavapai County. He was recognized as a broadminded man of sincerity and honesty of purpose. He strove to obliterate sectional hatred in the old territory and his every act was towards promoting industrial interests, no matter what locality was affected. In one speech in the assembly, he made this remark: "We must bring capital into Arizona, and we must enact laws to encourage investment on a basis of liberality and sincerity of purpose; after we get a foothold, we must still further encourage the advancement of Arizona."

The Exchange Saloon was a wooden building located on the northwest corner of Gurley and Granite St. in Prescott. It burned during the 1900 fire. "Billy" Mulvenon rebuilt on that site in 1901. The lower floor of the Mulvenon Building was divided by a staircase for 2 business locations prior to the recent 1990 remodeling. Various businesses occupied half of the lower floor, and the other half was occupied by the Gurley Street Bar.

Billy's brother Alexander V. Mulvenon was the bartender and a resident of the building until he died in 1907. The upper floor was originally a hotel with 6 similar furnished rooms. For a while, the building was rumored to house a collection of women "notoriously abandoned to lewdness."

Since 1991, the Gurley Street Grill has occupied the remodeled building.

William "Billy" Mulvenon was a determined man who was relentless in pursuing outlaws. The three people who led him into Nevada and all the way to Idaho have no such histories to tell.

Jessie Clevenger was an adopted child, with no history except her brief life with the Clevenger's. The Rio Las Pinos, La Plata, Colorado, USA Census of 1880 names her Jessie May Clevenger, age 7. Her historical story began when her parents were murdered and she was taken away by outlaws.

Mr. and Mrs. Clevenger and their daughter, Jessie, were only passing through the state of Arizona. There were no family members or close friends, who came to Prescott to be beside Jessie, during the trial. She was a stranger in town and had to endure the situation alone, except for the new friends who helped her. When she testified in court, there were no character witnesses for her, so part of her testimony was set aside, replaced by Frank Wilson's confession.

She must have despaired, knowing what happened, testifying what happened and yet, not being believed. Discovering she was pregnant at such a young and tender age would have been a shock, but to know that her kidnapper was the father, would have put a twist to her motherly joy. Frank Wilson was in his thirties, much older than the young Jessie. She had not chosen him to be her partner, but in spite of that, she seemed to care about him. Some might say this was a classic case of Stockholm syndrome, that can occur in 8% of kidnapping cases and consists of strong emotional ties that develop between two persons where one person intermittently harasses, beats, threatens, abuses, or intimidates the other.

Frank Wilson, according to his own confession, was using an alias, so there's no way to know who he really was. His historical story began when he joined Clevenger's party and was eventually hanged for the crime he confessed he alone committed. One report claimed that he had been indicted in Graham County for horse stealing and that Samuel Clevenger helped him out of that scrape.

From all the various testimonies and newspaper stories, it seems evident that he formed a stronger relationship with Jessie then that of just a captor. He must have cared for her if he kept her with him all the way up into Idaho. If he was afraid that she would identify him as a murderer, he could have killed her anywhere along the remote trail and buried the body, the same as he claimed he did to her parents. If he was a cold-blooded murderer, he could have easily disposed of her and made his escape much easier.

She became pregnant with his child and he kept her beside him when they settled in the small town of Oakley, ID before they were apprehended and taken back to Prescott to stand trial.

John A. Johnson had a little history. He said he was born in Trenton, New Jersey but was raised in Baltimore, where he had a wife and family, with a sister residing there. He was a member of the 10th Cavalry in Baltimore, Maryland before being assigned to the Territory and was discharged at Fort Thomas in February 1886, just prior to starting on the fatal journey with the Clevenger family. Before he was attached to Fort Thomas, his company was stationed at Fort Whipple, just outside of Prescott, AZ. It seems likely that he was already known in the community before his arrest. It might explain why there was a large committee of residents and civic leaders, who signed a petition to have his sentence commuted.

E15: Newly elected sheriff Bucky O'Neill

After he was released from prison, he never returned to his hometown where his family resided. He drifted around for a while, getting into petty scrapes with the law. At one point many years after the Clevenger murders, he returned to

Prescott for reasons unknown and was arrested for vagrancy and for threatening his landlady, a Mrs. Grisalda, in April 1907. His eventual fate is not known.

The mystery of those involved in the crime only adds to the allure of the missing money that has never been found. There are records that corroborate that Samuel C. Clevenger had a substantial amount of money from the sale of his ranch that he planned to use to start a new life in the Washington Territory. The fate of the lost money has never been acknowledged in any public record.

When Jessie confided the story about Samuel Clevenger burying the money each night while they traveled along the remote trail in the Buckskin Mountains, she was careful whom she trusted.

Jim Roberts was the brother of Mrs. Hartin, the kind woman who cared for Jessie. He and Jessie became good friends. At the time of these events, Jim was well known in the area. He was a soft-spoken man, not subject to idle conversation. He had a reputation as being very closed-mouthed and trustworthy even though he found himself in trouble from time to time.

He was involved in the Tewksbury/Pleasant Valley War in Yavapai County as a top gun where as many as fifty men died with their boots on in the feud that lasted several years. By the late 1880's, most of the leaders in the feud were dead. Jim

Roberts was among the living and was charged with murder along with the others who survived. No one was ever brought to trial because witnesses for the prosecution never showed up for trial.

Because of his fearless and brazen bravery, he went from being a wanted man to becoming a respected lawman. Newly elected sheriff Bucky O'Neill (following the retirement of William Mulvenon in 1889) hired Roberts as deputy sheriff. Jim Roberts' reputation and skill with firearms was much prized by the sheriff and civic leaders who wanted to bring law and order to the counties and communities.

The following April 1889, he was sent on a trip to the northern part of the county. The purpose of the trip was to assess the people in that part of the county, and to subpoena witnesses for the consideration of the case by the grand jury on May 5th of the four men held for robbing the Santa Fe train at Canyon Diablo on March 21, 1889.

The night he stopped at House Rock Valley, April 29, 1889, he met up with Harry Clayton, who carried the mail from Johnson, UT to Lee's Ferry. Clayton showed him the campsite where the crime was committed and told him about it.

Some of the charred bed clothing was still there, near several big rocks in the area, one in particular where the money had probably been buried.

Jim Roberts went to the mining town of Congress to help keep the peace and while there, he met twenty-two year old Melia Kirkland, the pretty daughter of pioneer rancher William Kirkland. Her father had raised the first American flag over Tucson in 1856. The couple were married in Prescott in 1891and took up residence in Jarome, AZ, a mining town perched on the side of Cleopatra Hill in the Verde Valley.

His confidential manner was esteemed by Jessie Clevenger, when she asked him to retrieve the buried money from the old campsite. As a gentleman who respected a confidential matter, he did as she asked, even though he came back empty handed. He never disclosed the secret she'd told him except to his brother, John Roberts.

When Jim Roberts was living in Jarome, he kept the peace even though it meant his life was on the line. One night, three men escaped to the outskirts of town after killing a man over a card game. They sent a challenge to the lawman Roberts, and a young deputy, to come and get them. As the two lawmen approached the desperados, Roberts said quietly to his deputy, "You take the one in the middle and I'll take the other two."

When the young deputy started to tremble, Roberts said in a kind but firm tone, *"Step out of the way son; I'll take 'em all."* A moment later, all three killers were dead on the ground.

Jim Roberts wasn't a man to brag and swag. He didn't drink or play poker and was known for living by the code of silence. He clammed up whenever anyone asked him about anything. Even his children were unfamiliar with their father's history, as he wouldn't talk about it.

Jessie couldn't have chosen a more qualified confidant.

Contradictions

While investigating the many diverse sources for this book, I discovered a few contradicting reports of incidents and thought I should share some of them here. Occasionally there is a contradiction of information from several sources that can only be resolved by common sense and more research. If I have hypothesized in my story, it is because the research implied the conclusion.

In this chapter, I'll present a few of these for your scrutiny.

Samuel C. Clevenger's name:

Samuel C. Clevenger was also referred to as J.W.Clevenger. A correct name for an individual is important in any historical research project. I've concluded the two names, as used in each instance, identify the same individual.

Jessie Clevenger's age:

Jessie Clevenger's age – Thirteen, fourteen, fifteen or seventeen; She is described as all four. The Rio Las Pinos, La Plata, Colorado, USA Census of 1880 states that Jessie was 7 years old, and that would make her 13-14 years old at the time of the murders. I can only commiserate her circumstance as tragic for any young woman.

Employment date for Johnson and Wilson:

Hiring of Johnson and Wilson – some reports say they were both hired at the same time, before the journey commenced from Fort Thomas. Other reports say that Johnson was hired while the Clevenger's still lived on their property to assist them in their preparations to leave. Later on, Wilson was hired when they reached the Phoenix area near Wickenburg, and Johnson vouched for him as an old acquaintance. He was taken on to guide them to the Washington Territory, and help care for the stock.

The date of the murders

The exact date that the murders were committed is unknown. There are reports that put it anywhere from the 20th of May to the 27th of May 1886. The court decided in accordance with the coroner's estimate of time of death to put the date as the 21st of May on the records of the court.

The murder of the Clevenger's:

John Roberts' record states that Jessie was sleeping in the tent when the men slipped in and killed the old people. She woke up terrified and begged for her life. They threatened to kill her if she told anyone.

Jessie's testimony as reported in the Arizona Champion newspaper states: She testified they were all in camp on the morning of the murder and that she was approaching the fire preparatory to making coffee when she saw Johnson, with his arms bare and an ax in hand, strike old man Clevenger down. He fell forward into the fire. She fled but looking back, she saw Johnson pull him from the fire and drag Clevenger's body round the tent. As Johnson struck Clevenger, he said, "You old s-n of a b---h, you have lived long enough!" After Jessie had run some distance, she said she heard Mrs. Clevenger scream and call her. She started back only to hear the groans of the unfortunate woman who was being murdered in the tent by Wilson. While giving her evidence the girl was quite self-possessed and added, she lived with Wilson through fear. She stated that Wilson and Johnson divided the money immediately after the crime was committed and that after traveling together some distance, Johnson left them and went to Nevada.

Jessie's testimony is consistent throughout all the newspaper articles and the court proceedings Wilson's confession: "Wilson said that he alone committed the murders. Johnson was away from the camp and knew nothing." (Clifton Clarion)

His confession was printed in the Weekly Citizen. He said that after he committed the murders, he took the wagon and the rest of the stock and overtook Johnson on the road with the rest of the horses. He told Johnson that Clevenger and his wife had gone to Utah by another road with friends and that the Clevenger's had joined them in their camp to continue their journey by another route. They continued to Utah and when they reached Toquerville, Wilson traded off some of the horses. He said when Johnson asked him what Clevenger would say, Wilson told him he had killed them, and threatened Johnson that if he told anyone, Wilson would say that Johnson helped to kill them both.

Johnson said he left camp on a horse hunt on the morning of the murder when he was overtaken by Wilson and Jessie in the wagon. They told him the old people had gone to Utah by another route. He never saw them again. (Weekly Champion)

Another report in a newspaper claims the three remained together until they reached Carbondale where they parted company, Wilson taking Jessie with him. Before they separated, Wilson confessed to Johnson what he'd done, gave him $200 and a team of horses. He again threatened Johnson that if he told, Wilson would blame the crime on him.

Another interesting account of the crime was recorded by Will C. Barnes, a writer, newspaperman and respected prominent resident of Arizona. In his account he said the following:

"As I recall the Clevenger murder case, Cephas Perkins, a well-known cattleman of Holbrook, and who was a prominent witness for the territory at the trial of the two men at Prescott, writes that a party consisting of himself and a Mr. and Mrs. Graves followed the Clevenger party on the road to Utah from Lee's Ferry in May 1886. Perkins states that in the Buckskin Mountains they camped one night near the same spot where the Clevenger's had camped a few days before.

E16: Will C. Barnes

Perkins had some loose stock with him. The next morning while running them near the Clevenger's camp his saddle horse stepped to his knees into a soft place, stumbled and fell heavily with him. He mounted and rode on after the cattle, but later they examined the spot where the horse fell and found signs of a new made grave. A little exploring discovered the hand and part of a woman's head. They eventually unearthed the mutilated and burned bodies of the two old people. The party drove on to Kanab, reported what they had found and proceeded on their way to the west of St. George, Utah, where Perkins was to receive some cattle.

Coming back a few weeks later, when near Pipe Springs, Perkins met a sheriff from Utah looking for him with a warrant for murder. He found himself accused of the murder of his companions, Graves and his wife, due to the fact that an elderly man and woman had been killed along the road and Perkins had two such people with him on the road from Lee's Ferry. Having proved his innocence by the presence in life of the two Graves and wife, Perkins went on to House Rock Valley where he turned his cattle out for the winter and camped there. Mr. and Mrs. Graves left him there. This was in the fall of 1886."

This account is in variance to other accounts that were either printed or reported. I'm sure it is true, but I think the time element was somehow confused. It was interesting, though, that Mr. Perkins was accused of the murder. He must have been surprised when the Sheriff served him the warrant, especially since his good friends, the Graves, were alive and well!

The theft:

A few different reports about the theft of the money that Clevenger carried with him: A report in the Arizona Weekly stated: "The old people were buried and the party moved on, when Wilson and Johnson divided the money, $450 and afterwards, they divided the stock."

Also, reported by the Clifton Clarion: "Wilson murdered Clevenger and his wife with an ax. Wilson and Johnson then divided the stock and five hundred dollars, which Clevenger had with him. They buried the bodies."

The Arizona Champion reported: "Jessie said she was fearful for her life and lived with Wilson through fear. She said Johnson and Wilson divided the money immediately after the crime was committed and then traveled together some distance until Johnson left them and went to Nevada."

The Arizona Champion also reported as part of Wilson's confession he said that at parting, he gave Johnson $200 and a team of horses at the same time telling him how he had killed Clevenger and his wife and afterwards, robbed them.

The mention of the proceeds from the sale of Mr. and Mrs. Clevenger's property in Fort Thomas is conspicuously not mentioned. That is because no one knew what had happened to it at this time; Jessie Clevenger kept her secret.

The travels:

According to Sheriff Mulvenon, when he trailed them to Kanab, he learned that they had continued on to Bullionville, where they divided the stock, money and merchandise, before splitting up.

Jessie stated that they split up the $500, found in the tent, right after the murders and traveled across southern Utah on the long road toward Idaho, dodging towns along the way and traveling into Nevada. Johnson and Wilson parted ways at Bullionville, near Pioche, NV while Wilson and Jessie continued up the trail into Idaho where they rented a small house in Oakley located in the Shoshone area.

Wilson stated that they continued to Utah and when they reached Toquerville, he traded off some of the horses.

They could have first traded off some of the stock in Toquerville, UT (which is not too far from Carbondale, another location they were supposed to have stopped to sell some horses) and possibly herded the rest to Bullionville, near Pioche, NV. The road between these two places is almost all salt flats below the Great Salt Lake, and alkaline fields. It would be difficult to drive a herd of horses across that without carrying a good amount of feed and water along.

The Manhunt

There are a few different versions of how Sheriff Mulvenon tracked down the outlaws. One account states that he first trailed Wilson and Jessie to Idaho, took them into Pocatello, ID and left them there, Wilson in jail and Jessie lodged with a woman. He then went in search of Johnson, with the help of Mr. Perkins, who we previously mentioned as being accidently arrested for the murders simply because he was with friends who resembled the description of the Clevenger's.

I chose to build my story on the account that Sheriff Mulvenon went into Nevada first, found Johnson, and arrested him, locking him in a jail there. Then he went in search of Wilson and Jessie. After he found them, he returned to Nevada to pick up Johnson. There is a record of a hotel stay by the sheriff and Jessie in Nevada at approximately the right time period that supports this story.

There were certain parts of the first story that I liked better, for instance, the part where Sheriff Mulvenon finds Johnson and returns to Pocatello, where Wilson and Jessie are, in order to take the group back to Prescott on the railway. Every time I envision Jessie, riding in a wagon all the way back to Prescott as in the other story while she is pregnant, it seems harsh.

Sometimes when different accounts report completely different information, you can usually study all the accounts out and they will eventually mesh into one story. I wasn't able to do that with these two dissimilar accounts of the manhunt. Some newspapers glorified the manhunt and probably simply didn't know the details, so they assumed a scenario. Readers were anxious for the particulars of the case and the newspapers were under pressure to provide something.

There's also the possibility that the witnesses who were interviewed gave conflicting information.

The location of the lost treasure

There are a few instances that refer to a "great deal of money carried by Clevenger on the journey", some, actual court documents. The knowledge of the sale of the property in Arizona begs the conclusion that he had more money with him. The $500 that was stolen on the day of the murders was from the sale of his water and ditch rights and there is a known bill of sale to vouch for that money. What happened to all the other money?

Jessie confided that her adopted father buried it the night before he was killed. She described the indicated location as far as she remembered old man Clevenger telling her about it the night before. Was she listening intently to his description or was she half-asleep? Did she hear, "by a large rock" and "dug a hole" and then just assumed it was the rock by the road?

It's completely logical to believe that a lot of money is missing. From the activities of those involved in this story, the misconceptions, the lies and the emotional entanglements, it is a recipe for treasure sleuths.

I have read all the testimonies, the conflicting statements, and have chosen whom to believe and will share that with you at the end of this book. You need to make a choice also. Only then, will the story come together to lead you to the buried treasure.

Washington Territory or Idaho

The original Washington Territory of 1886 encompassed the present boundary between the United States and Canada (the 49th parallel). On the admission of the State of Oregon to the union in 1859, the eastern portions of the Oregon Territory, including southern Idaho, portions of Wyoming west of the continental divide, and a small portion of present-day Ravalli County, Montana were annexed to the Washington Territory. Idaho grew in population after gold was discovered in 1860 and, in 1863, became its own territory called Idaho Territory. It was many years later, on July 3, 1890, that Idaho joined the Union. The use of the term of Idaho in many reports of 1886 can be confusing.

Frank Wilson's Name

Frank Wilsons' name was spelled with one "L" in all the court documents. When Wilson signed his own name on a document, he spelled it with two "L's", Willson. He claimed that Frank Wilson was not his real name. Did he purposely misspell it when he signed, or was it truly his real name?

Horse stealing incident in Graham County

There is a record of arrest made in December, 9, 1884, in Graham County for the following:

Frank Wilson, "on a charge of having in his possession, with intent to consent to his own use, the property of the

United States: to rid, one horse furnished, and to be used for the military service of the United States of Graham County." There was also the same exact charge against S.C. Clevenger and J.B. Collins (the man who purchased Clevenger's property). All three were charged and posted bail. Looks like they all served time in the slammer together.

Jar vs. can vs. pot?

The baking-powder can, recently invented at that time may have been used as a place to stash cash, as is claimed in many stories of buried treasure including earlier accounts of this story. Some usual containers to hide cash were jars made of glass or ceramic with tight fitting lids, or pots made of metal with loose lids or tin boxes. It is reported that Jesse James buried 1880 Morgan dollars and gold pieces in mason jars that were later dug up. If Samuel C. Clevenger was a smart man, he would protect his money when he buried it in the dirt and would conceal it inside one of the above choices.

The Route

When it comes to the route the Clevenger's traveled, we have two conflicting stories. One story comes from a mysterious map drawn on a notepad with the name Randall on it along with the initials E.M.T. This notepad has mysteriously disappeared. The map showed the alleged route going through

Globe, Show Low and then to Tuba City. The other account is from John Roberts (Jim's Brother), who was very close to Jessie, and goes into detail about stops along the way, money spent, etc. His account took the Clevenger's through Phoenix, Chino Valley and up through Flagstaff. The reason people have conflicts with Robert's route primarily focuses on three items:

1. There was not a route to cross the Colorado River;

2. The distance 600+ miles would have been difficult to travel in the timeframe specified;

3. The name of the ferryman at Lee's Ferry was not correct.

In my research, I was able to validate and answer each of these concerns. I was able to prove that pioneers crossed the Little Colorado River at Grand Falls. As a matter of fact, this was a very popular crossing and just a little Northeast of Flagstaff. As for travel time, I was able to demonstrate that a party moving horses could easily cover 20 miles a day versus a party moving cattle would estimate only about 10 miles a day. When considering this, the Clevengers had more than enough time to cover the route through Phoenix. The final issue was with the ferryman at Lee's Ferry that Roberts had specified in his account. In my research, I was able to validate the ferryman, Warren Johnson, had convinced his brother-in-law, David Brinkerhoff, to be his partner at the ferry for approximately five years. This places Brinkerhoff at the ferry and confirms the statement in Robert's account.

I am more convinced that they traveled the route specified in Roberts account based on the current information we have.

The Roberts Account

The Roberts account or more formally known as the "Arizona Historical Review" by John Roberts has been debated for several reasons, specifically the inaccurate information contained within it. The account was written in 1930, 44 years after the murders. It would be hard for Roberts or anyone for that matter to recollect the details of the Clevenger account with perfect accuracy at such an old age and with so many years past since the event. Not to mention Roberts was giving an account of what his brother, Jim, encountered. A few mistakes is not reason enough to dismiss the entire account. The items debated in the account are things that I feel could have been easily confused or overlooked due to old age. For example, in his account, he says the Clevenger's were on their way to Idaho. This is not in harmony with other accounts that say the Clevenger's were going to Washington Territory. Considering Wilson and Jessie were eventually discovered in Idaho this could have been a simple mistake. He also misjudged the dates of Jessie's pregnancy, something a man might struggle with. You might ask why the Roberts account even matters. Why is it so important? This is one of the only accounts that stated that Samuel Clevenger was traveling with more money than the $500 he carried on his person. The amount of money mentioned in Roberts account could be valued very high today. If it is in fact true, then Samuel Clevenger had additional money he carried with him on his journey northward and that money is possibly near a campsite on the summit of the Buckskin Mountains just 15 miles Southeast of Kanab, UT, With a simple search using a modern day metal detector you might be the one to stumble upon it and cash in.

Clevenger's Wealth

Multiple reports say Clevenger had between $2,000 and $6,000. Tax records of 1884. state he had "2 houses, furniture, improvements on the ranch near Camp Thomas, 37 cattle, 3 horses, 2 mules, 2 wagons, harness, saddle, Misc. all valued at a total $2,174. This value almost doubles when sold, ($4,348). There were also 160 Acres he homesteaded in La Plata, Colorado. He had applied for a homestead deed that was awarded in 1888 and we are not sure if he was renting this property out or planning on returning to it. When you take all his assets into consideration we can assume he was carrying with him a good amount of money.

Location of the Clevenger's Grave

The location of the Clevenger's gave site is unknown. The Deseret News article dated March 9, 1887, written by James S. Emett states: *'and, (after holding an inquest and doing everything possible to discover the perpetrators) buried them in the Kanab cemetery.'* The problem is, at the time, there were two Kanab Cemeteries and Emett didn't specify which one. Kanab's main cemetery (east) has pretty good detailed records going back well beyond these murders and there are no records of them in the main cemetery.

Since Zadock was the sextant of the north cemetery, he may have buried them there. Only the official "Inquest" will tell the whole story, but unfortunately, this record has been lost. James S. Emett is the man who took over Lee's Ferry operation for the Mormon Church following Warren Marshall Johnson.

The north cemetery fell into disrepair and most of the headstones were destroyed.

There are no surviving records of the cemetery on the north end of town. It is called the Pioneer Cemetery only because of its location near the Pioneer Park. This cemetery operated at the same time as the main cemetery on the east end of Kanab. At the time of the Clevenger murders, it was still in service and its sextant was Zadock Knapp Judd, the same man who conducted the official Inquest.

Lost and found Treasures

Arizona is alive with legends of lost treasures, including the famous Lost Dutchman's Gold Mine. There are accounts of parts of that treasure being found in the past. For being such a vast amount of gold, (as reported), some of it certainly should have turned up by now!

Stories of hidden treasure in Arizona began with Coronado's search for the Seven Cities of Cibola in 1540. He was looking for a city of gold but only found Native American mud huts. Missing loot from train robberies abound in Arizona legend. Indian gold from South America is described as making its way into North America and Arizona and hidden away in caves. Even though Arizona mines produced an abundance of silver – there were few that contained gold – and yet stories of a profusion of lost gold mines are recorded and passed down.

There seems to be plentiful stories of lost treasure which is a fascinating and rich history to explore. Along with each legend is a tale that explains what really happened. The best ones are those discovered in old family histories or written down and recorded by modern relatives.

Many years ago, when I was very young, my dad was an avid metal detectorist. We lived in Utah up near the Uintah Mountains near the old hangouts of Butch Cassidy and the Sundance Kid.

An old cabin called Josie's Cabin located on Split Mountain near Jensen, Utah, was an outlaw hangout. Old Josie Steward would let them stay there in return for the money and help that they occasionally gave her. The whole area benefitted from the outlaws who stayed in Brown's Hole, when they were hiding out from the law. The stories of buried treasure and stolen loot throughout that area were numerous.

My dad was invited by his friend, Dave, to metal detect the yard of their old homestead. The place had been abandoned for years and the property was being currently used as an old apple orchard. The place was finally sold to a company who planned to bulldoze the house and plow up the grounds to cover with asphalt for a parking lot. The destruction was to begin in two days and Dave had permission to look for any family heirlooms that might be left in the old place.

Dave said that there was an old legend in their family that a gallon jar of gold coins had been buried in the apple orchard a hundred years ago by his great, great grandfather. One night, the old man had suddenly died before he could disclose the spot where he'd buried the money. That jar full of gold was the legacy that he wanted to leave for his family. If he had ever drawn a map, no one ever found it. Over the years, relatives would go dig in the apple orchard, but the gold was never discovered.

My dad went over to help Dave search for the gold early one morning. The apple orchard was big and he and Dave started with a grid to mark the area. They assumed it was probably buried beside a tree, so they searched around as many old trees as they had time to look. My dad always felt like the gold was there, but they couldn't find where it was buried since they were unable to search the whole orchard. If they'd had more time, he was sure it could be found.

Before they finished with the orchard, Dave asked him to search inside the empty old house. My dad went into the attic and ran the detector along the walls and ceiling. He was surprised to get a reading along the old wooden floor. He and Dave pulled up the boards and were amazed at what they found.

Secreted inside the hidden compartment in the floor were several old guns in new-like condition. There were guns that dated from the Civil War, some from the first WW and a few newer ones. There were a total of five guns hidden inside the old house that was scheduled to be demolished.

Dave was astonished to discover the hidden arsenal and had never heard family stories of anything like this being concealed in the house. After they finished searching the rest of the house, they went back out to the apple orchard. They ran out of time before they could discover the buried loot.

The new parking lot that was built over the orchard has a gold stash buried beneath it. Maybe someday, the lot will be dug up for another reason, and some lucky person will stumble over a gallon jar filled with gold coins!

That is the kind of treasure story that is interesting and worth pursuing. The gold will stay buried or hidden or stashed wherever it lays until someday, someone finds it!

You might be curious if my dad and his friend ever told anyone about the hidden guns stashed in the attic that they had found? No, they didn't. Dave kept the treasure as a family heirloom.

Another time, my dad was asked to help find a lost treasure that had been missing for 65 years. There was an elderly woman named Harriett, who lived out of town on an old farm. When she and her husband were first married, he built the house where they lived. They had stayed there, while he farmed the land around the house and raised their children.

Her husband had passed away a few years ago and she lived there alone. There were many wonderful memories that kept Harriett in her old house. There was also a token lost for 65 years that she had been looking for, ever since it was lost.

Shortly after Harriett and her husband moved into their new house, she was expecting their first child. While he plowed the fields that spring, she was busy in the front yard planting bulbs. It was an arduous job because of her condition. While she hurriedly dug holes in the dirt, she brushed the clumps off her hands before moving on to the next bed. All morning she worked until it was time to prepare lunch. She went inside and washed her hands. That was when she discovered her little diamond wedding ring was missing.

Harriett rushed back outside and looked everywhere that she had been working, but she could not find the ring. As the years passed, there was a tentative search for the ring by her husband and children. Even the grandchildren kept a sharp eye out, but it was never found.

It was time for Harriett to move into an assisted care home due to deteriorating health and she thought about her ring still lost in the yard. My dad took his metal detector over and within a few hours, he had found the missing treasure!

The best part about this story isn't the discovery of the ring. The best part is the story that led up to its discovery. I believe *that* is the lost treasure that now is found. The ring can be handed down to her descendants along with the wonderful story of the many years it was missing, the meaning of the ring and what it stood for; the yearning to find it by a young woman who grew older each day.

We don't always hear about the treasure stories when the hidden wealth is found. Sometimes it's necessary to keep the secret! Just because you can't find a mass of stories about numerous individuals finding bars of gold, doesn't mean it never happened.

When people disparage treasure hunting, they have no idea how much fun it can be. Not only might you actually find a treasure, but you will definitely discover a story full of intrigue, mystery and great human interest. Every treasure hunt needs to be researched extensively. You will find clues that will lead in the right direction.

There are clues to the lost Clevenger Gold in this book, a story well reported, well researched and analyzed. You might be the one person who can figure out where the money is. The next chapter will give you my theory about what really happened and where the treasure is now.

Secret of Clevenger's Gold

A ton of research goes into locating a hidden stash that has been missing for one hundred and thirty years and lost for so long. This story is especially intriguing because it is based on a secret kept by a young girl.

As an orphan during that time, she was likely used like a slave when she went to live with Mr. and Mrs. Clevenger. It wasn't unusual in the early days after the great civil war, to adopt a child to simply use as a pair of hands to take care of things. If she was provided a roof over her head, three meals a day (even if she had to cook them) and a bed, she should be grateful.

If poor Jessie was looking for loving parents or siblings, she was robbed of those in her life. She had an adoptive mother who was sick and needed to be cared for. I imagine that was why old man Clevenger agreed to adopt a girl. To him, she was a servant to care for his sick wife; otherwise, he would have adopted a boy to work for him.

When the outlaws kidnapped her, she was forced to exchange one bad situation for another. Jessie must have been adaptable, because she did as Wilson bid her to do. She had been trained to obey. Wilson treated her differently than Clevenger had. He might have been gentler and kind, after all, he had defended her when she was abused by Samuel Clevenger. Jessie probably never expected to be treated special by anyone, and because of that kind of innocence, that tolerant nature and her naturally selfless attitude, she didn't hold others to a standard of expectation.

One moment, she was a child in servitude to the man and woman who had provided her with a home. The next moment, she was a woman who was kidnapped by an outlaw who made new demands on her.

Frank Wilson had been traveling with Jessie and her parents for several months. He had seen her abuse and defended her. He was a man who didn't put down roots, a type of loner who was only looking to move on to the next opportunity. I imagine the women in his life were only there for a good time.

Maybe Wilson had been raised in a good home, with a God-fearing upbringing and a loving family. Something in his past gave him a strong conscience and desire for redemption. Something else drew him away from that solid secure womb and enticed him into an opposite purpose. Whatever it was, it compelled him to hide from those who were part of his past. He seemed to live his life recklessly, with abandon of values and in retaliation of forced ideals.

There may have been something about Jessie that took his mind back to a gentler time in his life, a remembrance of family that he'd abandoned but never forgotten; a link with part of his heart.

When he watched her being abused, maybe something snapped inside of him. When he and Johnson murdered the parents, they could both have had strong personal reasons for doing what they each did. It couldn't have been planned, or they would have done a better job of hiding their crime. It was a crime of passion for two different reasons. Johnson had his reason and Wilson did, too.

When Jessie visited him in jail, she was passionate in her feelings of disappointment and hurt that he had confessed to both murders. Wilson seemed to accept his fate – guilty of one murder – why not confess to both and save Johnson's neck? Would that redeem his past deeds?

Jessie must have felt very alone after Wilson was hung. After all, she had spent many months with him. Her life had involved only her adoptive parents, caring for her sick mother at an isolated ranch far out in the San Pedro of the Territory of Arizona and doing her father's bidding. We don't know what all he might have demanded of her. Whatever she had to endure, she was always submissive and obedient.

Had she ever had a friend? It sounds unlikely. Was Wilson her first friend? It certainly could have started that way.

Her baby was born a few weeks later and her heart must have been torn between loving her baby and resenting how it was conceived. If she cared for Wilson, she may have looked at her child with love in her eyes.

She kept her baby for eighteen months before placing her up for adoption. There was no way for her to provide a living for the child. She was almost a child herself. She couldn't live with Mrs. Hartin forever.

Back in those days, respectable women didn't work for pay. There were very few positions for a woman, and the standards for obtaining them were high. For instance, being a schoolteacher was an acceptable way for a woman to support herself, but she was in competition with men who had families to support. Most widowed ladies went to live with a relative after they found themselves alone.

What choices did Jessie have? She was uneducated, not a widow, and her reputation was tarnished for life.

Maybe that was when she started to think about the money buried up on the mountain. If she had wanted the money before, she could have told Wilson. She could have told Sheriff Mulvenon. For some reason, she didn't want anything to do with that money, until she was faced with the decision to place her daughter up for adoption because she couldn't support her.

It was exactly at the time she was about to let her baby go, that she asked Jim Roberts to go find the money. I think she was desperate and she set aside her personal feelings – maybe her abhorrence at what happened at that campsite where the money was buried. Maybe she considered it dirty money, or cursed in some way. Whatever the reason, she never wanted it until she had to give up her baby.

If Jessie was used like a slave by old man Clevenger, maybe she didn't want anything to do with his money. She may have felt that it wasn't hers to keep. She was young and probably not well educated. Perhaps she had been taught to be honest and scrupulous in her dealings when she was at the orphanage. The fact that she waited so long to disclose the location of the money indicates that she didn't consider it belonged to her.

She was also married right after she gave up her baby. I imagine there weren't very many men who wanted to marry a woman who had been kidnapped by outlaws, held captive for months, and given birth to an outlaw's baby. I expect all the folks who cared for her wanted her to marry someone and be happy. Maybe her future husband had a condition before he would marry her. The sight of the child might have angered him and Jessie might have been pressured to place her up for adoption in order to marry.

The buried money could have helped her escape many fates and would allow her to keep her beloved daughter. Being an orphan herself, she probably cared deeply that she raise her own child. If she had never wanted the buried money before, she now had important reasons for it to be found.

She couldn't go find it herself. That would require a horse, supplies and an escort. Women didn't travel alone in those days. She had to find another way to get the money so she searched out a trustworthy person to help.

It must have been a heartbreaking moment for Jessie when Jim returned empty handed. She had no choice but to give up her child and marry the man who would have her. Even sadder is the fact that her baby died a year and a half later.

If she could have lived out her life with Wilson, she probably would have been happy. I'm sure she must have felt that he wanted her. No one had ever wanted her before and he was the first. She probably loved him in her own way.

Since he refused to be whom he really was, his true identity put behind him, the relationship with Jessie suited him. He could pretend with her because she didn't care who he was. She was the rare person who did not expect special treatment in life and did not expect others to favor her in any way. If not for the murder, they might have had a happy life. If not for the murder of those old people, he might have settled down somewhere with Jessie and started a new life.

It's possible that the only crime Wilson wanted to commit was robbery. He and Johnson had planned to rob the Clevenger's, steal the $500 stashed in the tent, steal two horses and ride off before sunrise. They had been traveling with the older couple for months, had watched Samuel Clevenger reach into his money belt and pay for supplies. The last time he pulled money out was when they were crossing Lee's Ferry. By then both Johnson and Wilson would be tired of having no money. They would also have realized what an easy target old man Clevenger was. There was no one to protect him from being robbed.

Johnson may have been tired of being treated poorly by his boss. After all, he was a soldier who had served his country and deserved more respect. If he was ordered to start to work that morning, and possibly called, "boy", he could have resented Samuel Clevenger's prejudicial treatment and in a fit of rage, while chopping wood for the morning fire, turned and hit the old man with the ax.

Wilson was nearby and saw what happened. He understood Johnson's anger, had seen it building over the last few months. He grabbed the ax from Johnson and when Mrs. Clevenger began to scream, he meant to knock her unconscious but hit her too hard and it killed her. He tried to clean up the scene, ordering Johnson to strip out of his bloodied clothes and throw them into the fire, while he laid the ax into the flames to burn off the blood.

The fear on Jesse's face would have motivated him to move faster, bury the bodies, burn the bloodied bedding. He might have even been afraid that Johnson would hurt Jessie, so he demanded she come with them, under threat of death.

Without thinking clearly, he only wanted to escape and run as far away as possible. The hastily buried bodies, the clumsy fire, the lack of a good plan of escape all point to people who were in a panic to escape.

When the group reached Nevada, clearly Wilson didn't want to stay with Johnson, so he and Jessie went their own way. He wasn't very good at covering his tracks or trying to hide out. I would guess this was his first attempt at avoiding capture for such a serious crime. In his past misdemeanors, he simply changed his name, bought his way out or played a card game of chance, hoping for one more gamble.

After months of living in Idaho, Wilson began to relax and feel safe. Once again, he could have moved on, left Jessie behind, and saved himself from a future hanging.

The night that Sheriff Mulvenon finally found them, it was said they were dining. This could have been a special occasion for the couple, as Jessie might have just concluded she was with child and shared the news with Wilson.

Wilson had evaded his past for many years, but this new situation would give him pause to consider melding the past and the future, now that he was to be a father. Was it possible to reconcile the two?

Whatever reasons Jessie had for keeping her secret about the money buried somewhere in the Buckskin Mountains, we will never know. We can only speculate. I think it's important, though, to know the reason she finally decided to disclose what she knew about the hidden money. We have certain facts about her situation and can deduce some possible motives. I think she was desperate; more desperate then when she was with Wilson because she never told him about the buried cash.

The money is still there, buried beside a large rock along an old wagon road somewhere in the Buckskin Mountains. Nearby would be an indentation in the ground that had once held two bodies. When the midnight moon shines bright enough, the shadows of the past gently sway as in days forgotten. By now, the winds would have reshaped the landscape and molded the hillsides into new contours.

The ghosts of buried treasure hang on to their hard-earned caches. Old man Clevenger might still be sitting by the invisible campfire, watching out for his stash of buried loot. His vigilant eyes shine in the dark, while he waits, alert through the murky night for intruders.

When you are wandering those hills under the nighttime sky and you see a lone old man staring into vanishing flames, look past him to the couple who stand nearby, hand in hand.

Wilson and Jessie are watching too.

E17

The Legend of Clevenger's Lost Gold

TIMELINE OF EVENTS
Related to Clevenger's Murder and Missing Treasure

March 1-14th, 1886
The Clevenger's sell their ranch near Fort Thomas AZ. Receives around $2,150, plus $500 for his water/ditch rights, along with 25-30 horses. They depart on their journey and hire John A. Johnson to assist.

Month of April, 1886
The Clevenger Party arrives at the Orlando Ranch a few miles outside of Phoenix where he hires Frank Wilson to help with journey.

April – May, 1886
Clevenger party leaves the Orlando Ranch and proceeds to travel toward Flagstaff. Frank Wilson plans a route avoiding largely populated communities.

Early May, 1886
- Reach Lee's Ferry for crossing
- Secret talks between Wilson and Johnson

May, (approximately, May 18th) 1886
- Reach the Buckskin Mountains
- Samuel Clevenger buries money each night, fearful that it might be stolen from him by his hired hands.

May 21, 1886
- Settle into campsite in Buckskin Mountains
- The murder of Samuel and Charlotte Clevenger
- Johnson and Wilson divide the $500

May 25-27 (approximate), 1886
- Sell off part of stock or the whole herd
- Head for Pioche, NV

June 6-10 (approximate), 1886
- Johnson and Wilson along with Jessie, part ways in Pioche, NV
- Wilson and Jessie travel up into Idaho

October, 1886
The bodies of Samuel and Charlotte Clevenge are found buried in the Buckskin Mountains.

January, 1887
Sheriff Mulvenon tracked down the outlaws and arrested them for the murders.

June, 1887
The trial for the murder is held

August 12, 1887
Frank Wilson is hung in Prescott, AZ for the murders, while John A. Johnson is reprieved until Sept. 23rd.

September 23, 1887
John Johnson is sentenced to life in prison. After serving 6 years, he is released and pardoned for the crime.

February, 1889
- Jessie is faced with decision to have to give up her baby
- Asks Jim Roberts to go dig up the money

April 29, 1889
- Jim Roberts looks for buried money in Buckskin Mountains
- Returns empty handed

May, 1889
- Jessie marries John Speer and moves to Colorado

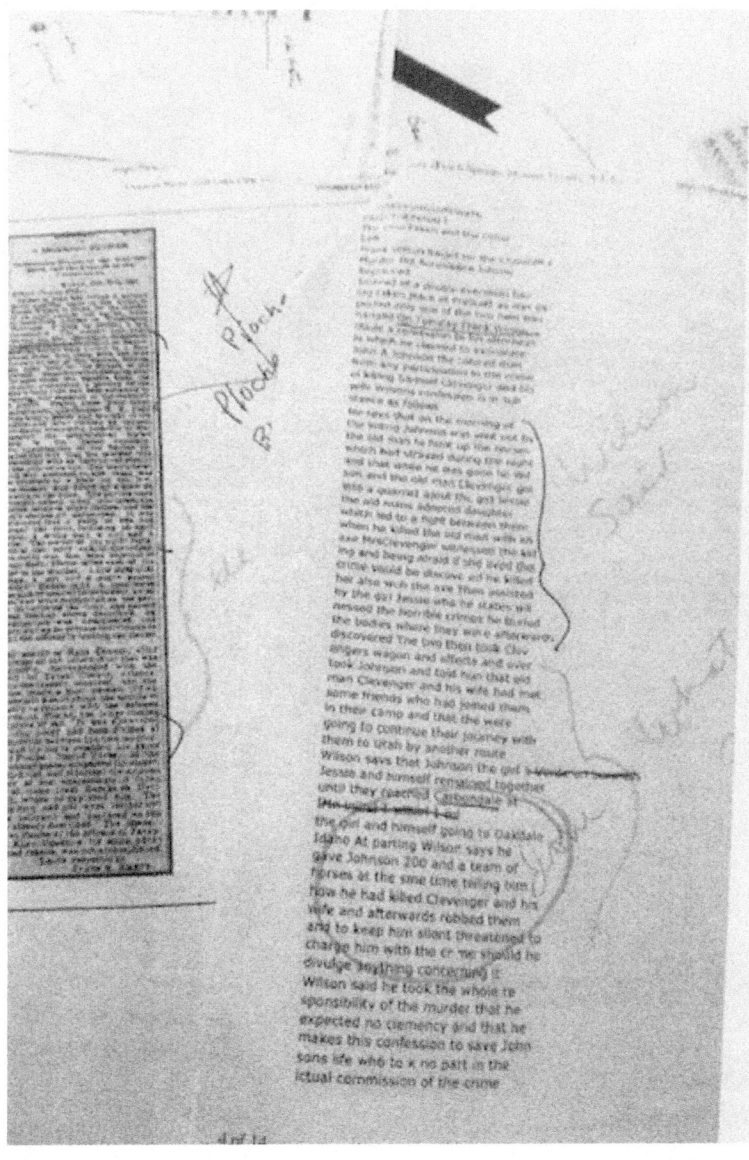

In the District Court of the First Judicial District of the Territory of Arizona, in and for the County of Pima, sitting etc.

The United States of America,

versus

Jerome B. Collins.

Personally appeared before me, W. F. Fitzgerald, Judge of the above entitled Court, on this 17th day of October, A.D. 1885, Jerome B. Collins as principal, and W M Griffith and Henry E Lacy as sureties, who each duly acknowledged himself indebted to the United States of America in the sum of One thousand five hundred dollars, lawful money of the United States, to be levied of his goods and chattels, lands and tenements, and for the payment of which well and truly to be made, they and each of them, respectively, hereby binds himself, his heirs, executors and administrators, jointly and severally, firmly by these presents.

The condition of the above obligation is such, that Whereas, the United States Grand Jury, called and sitting as such, at the regular September term of the above entitled Court, and on or about the 17th day of October, 1885, did find and present to the above entitled Court, in the manner and form as required by law, an indictment against the above bounden Jerome B. Collins, charging him with violating Section 5438 of the Revised Statutes of the United States.

Now, therefore, if the above named John B. Collins, shall appear and answer said charge, in the above entitled Court, and shall at all times hold himself amenable to the orders and processes of said Court, and shall if convicted, appear for judgment and render himself in execution thereof, then the above obligation to be void, otherwise to remain in full force and effect.

Signed and sealed this 17th day of October, 1885.

Jerome B. Collins
W M Griffith
Henry E Lacy

Territory of Arizona,
County of Pima.   ss.   W M Griffith and Henry E Lacy the

persons whose names are subscribed as sureties to the above recognizance, being severally sworn, each for himself says, that he is a resident and householder within the county of Pima, and Territory of Arizona, and that he is worth the amount specified in said recognizance as the penalty thereof over and above all his just debts and liabilities, exclusive of property exempt from execution.

Subscribed and sworn to before me
this 17th day of October, 1885.

C. S. Clifford, Clerk

W M Griffith
Henry E Lacy

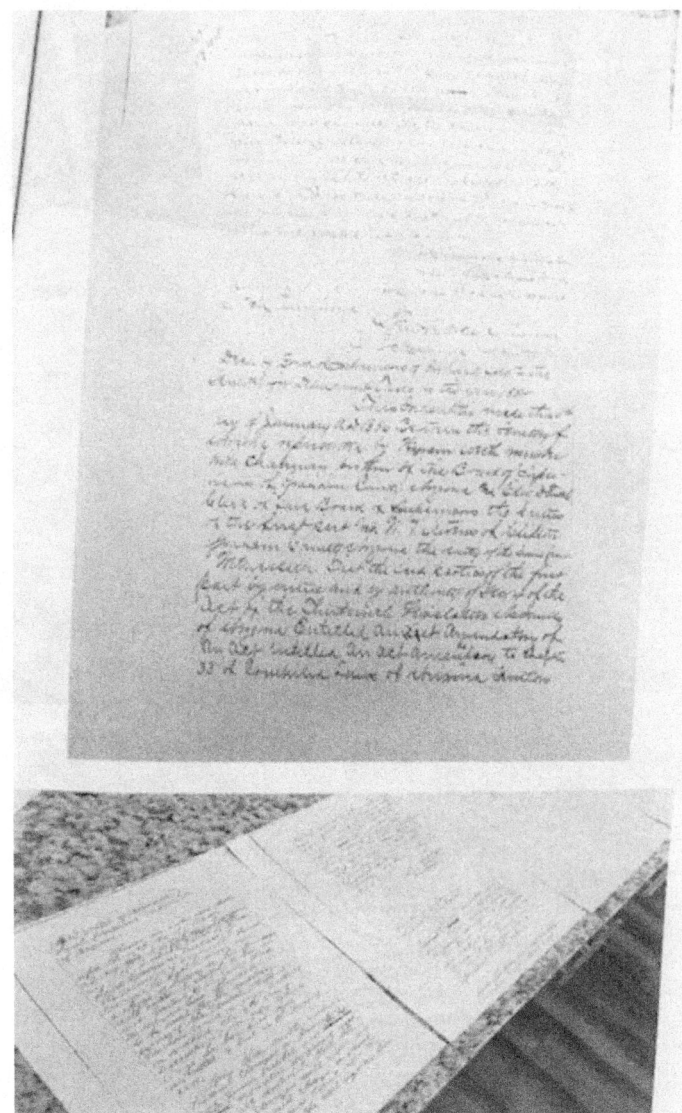

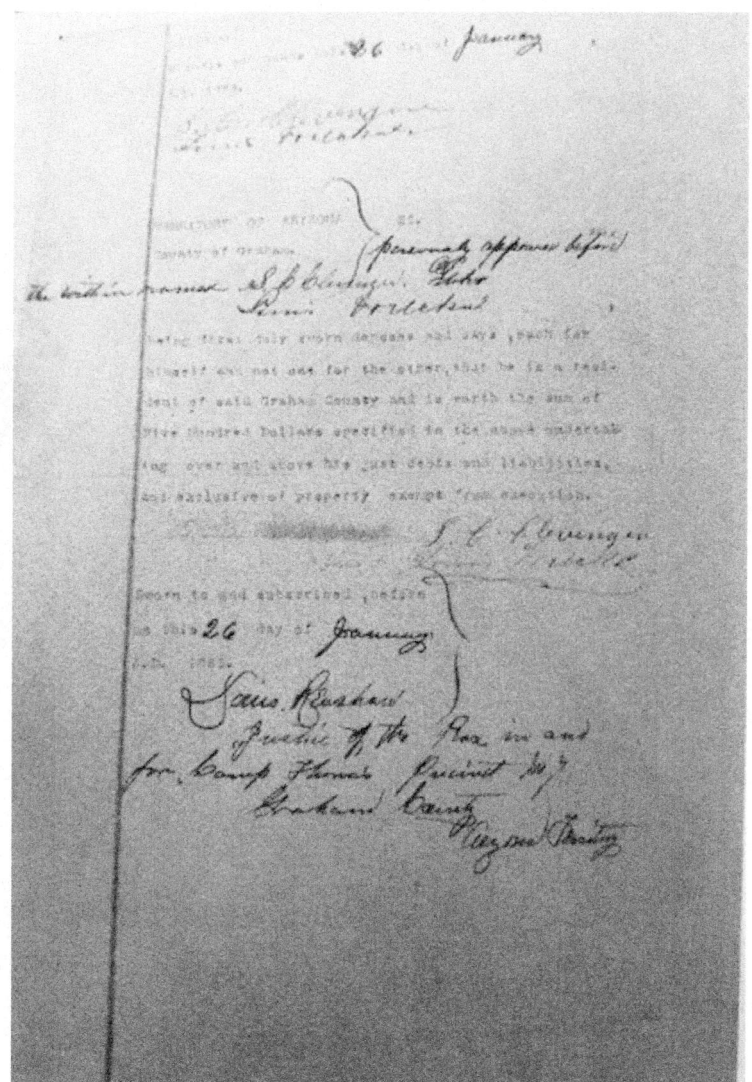

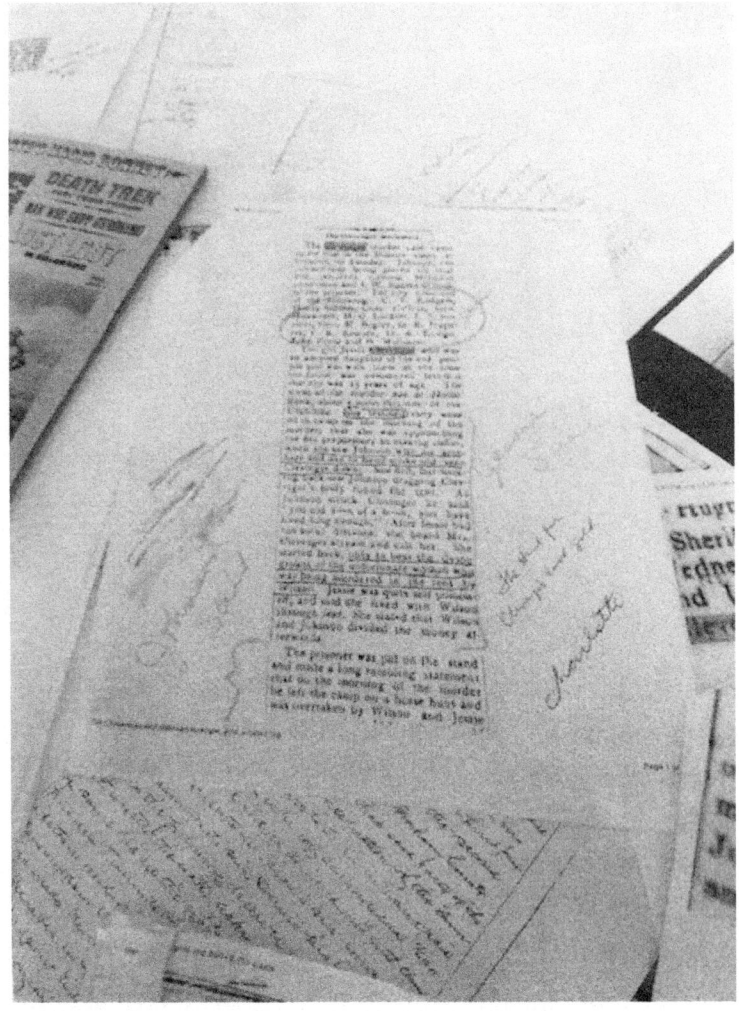

COMING SOON

"The Hunt For Clevenger's Lost Gold"

I will soon be releasing a new fiction novel called "The Hunt for Clevenger's Lost Gold". The story follows three teenage boys in the year 1933 as they set out on an adventure to find Clevenger's treasure. Full of adventure and danger, the story provides a fun way for the entire family to learn about Clevenger's Lost Gold in a fictional fascinating story setting.

FOLLOW THE CLEVENGER GOLD STORY

www.ClevengersGold.com

Video's, Podcasts, Documents, Maps & More!

References

Information for this book was obtained from various and numerous newspaper accounts of the events of 1886-1887 concerning the murder of Mr. and Mrs. Clevenger.

- The Clifton Clarion (Clifton, Graham County, A.T., AZ)
- Weekly Citizen
- Apache County (AZ) Critic
- Phoenix (AZ) Herald
- Prescott (AZ) Morning Courier
- St. Johns (AZ) Herold
- Arizona Weekly Journal Miner (AZ)
- Arizona Weekly Champion

- Arizona Weekly Citizen
- The Arizona Sentinel
- Deseret News (SLC)
- The Daily Courier, (AZ)
- Salt Lake Herald (UT)
- The University of Arizona University Libraries
- Arizona Historical Review by John Roberts
- Account written by Will C. Barnes on January 5, 1930, a prominent resident of AZ from 1880 to 1899, and eyewitness to the hanging of Wilson.
- Prescottazhistory.blogspot.com by Drew Desmond
- Yavapai County Countable Prescott Precinct History
- True West Magazine
- WikiVividly Yavapai County Sheriff's Office
- The Verde Independent
- Wikipedia
- American Cowboy Chronicles
- Arizona Memory Project
- Book: *The Grave of Sheriff William J. Mulvenon in Mountain View Cemetery* in Prescott by David Schmittinger

- www.officialdata.org Inflation Rate between 1886-2017 Inflation Calculaton

Illustrations

All images used by permission or from public domain.

- E1: Newspaper clipping. The Weekly Champion
- E2: Samuel & Sharlotte Clevenger, ka Frontier Magazine 1974
- E3: Newspaper clipping. The Clifton Clarion
- E4: Buffalo soldiers (public domain, wikipedia)
- E5: Skull in Desert Sand, Courtesy Ian Barbour (Flikr.com Creative Commons license)
- E6: Flagstaff Arizona Late 1800's (public domain, wikipedia)
- E7: Map of buckskin mountains, © 2018 Aaron Werner
- E8: Sheriff Mulvenon Courtesy of Sharlot Hall Museum Library & Archives / Leroy E. Eslow Photos / PC-4 7.2
- E9: Haskell Jolly, FamilySearch.org (Family Archives)
- E10: Jessie Clevenger True Frontier Magazine 1974

- E11: Jim Roberts (Photo: Southwest Studies Archives, Scottsdale Community College)
- E12: 1886 Silver and Gold Coins (creative commons – public domain)
- E13: 1886 Silver Certificate $1 (creative commons – public domain)
- E14: Photograph of treasure hunting group © 2018 Aaron Werner
- E15: Newly elected sheriff Buckey O'Neill commons.wikimedia.org (public domain)
- E16: Will C. Barnes commons. Wikimedia.org (public domain)
- E17: Cover Page, Gunslinger in the shadows © istockphoto.com
- E18: Photo of Aaron Werner by Daryl Young © 2018 Aaron Werner

Postscript

ARPA (Archaeological Resources Preservation Act.

RULES IMPLEMENTING A.R.S. 15-1631 and 41-841, ET SEQ. THE ARIZONA ANTIQUITIES ACT

8-201 General

A. Definitions: the following definitions shall apply in this Chapter unless the context requires otherwise:

    1. "Affinity" means the condition of relationship established through membership n a common cultural group.

    2. "Applicant" means an institution, organization or corporation organized for scientific, research, or land-use planning purposes that seeks to obtain a permit.

    3. "Archaeological site" means any area with material remains of past Indian or non-Indian life or activities that are of archaeological interest, including without limitation, historic or prehistoric ruins, burial grounds, and inscriptions made by human agency.

4. "Archaeological specimen" is defined in A.R.S. '41-841.

5. "Collect" means to remove an object from its location without disturbing the ground at or around that location.

6. "Collection survey" means a survey that may, but need not, involve the actual collection of archaeological or paleontological specimens.

7. "Director" means the Director of the Arizona State Museum or an official designee of the Director.

8. "Excavate" means to effect any disturbance of the ground, including movement of earth or stone

Policy Number: 8-201
Y Name: Rules Implementing A.R.S. '15-1631 and '41-841, et seq., The Arizona Antiquities Act –

General Policy Revision Dates: 6/91
Page 2
Rev. 5/00

9. "Excavation" means a field activity involving ground disturbance for the purpose of intensive examination of subsurface remains, including testing for the purpose of site evaluation.

10. "Explore" means to pursue any activity with the purpose of locating, recording or investigating any archaeological or paleontological site.

11. "Kinship" means the condition of relationship by traceable descent from a common ancestor.

12. "Lands owned or controlled by the State" means lands owned or controlled by the State of Arizona or by any agency, instrumentality or political subdivision of the State of Arizona, including any county or municipal corporation.

13. "Non-collection survey" means a survey that does not include the collection of archaeological or paleontological specimens.

14. "Paleontological site" means any area in which paleontological specimens are found.

15. "Paleontological specimen" means a fossilized plant or animal or fossilized evidence of a plant or animal such as a footprint.

16. "Permit" means an Arizona Antiquities Act Permit for Archaeological or Paleontological Investigations on Lands Owned or Controlled by the State as required by A.R.S. '41-841

17. "Permittee" means permanent protection from disturbance of an archaeological or paleontological site in situ, of scientific data recovery to preserve the information and specimens contained in the site.

18. "Preservation" means permanent protection from disturbance of an archaeological or paleontological site

in situ, of scientific data recovery to preserve the information and specimens contained in the site.

Policy Number: 8-201
Y Name: Rules Implementing A.R.S. '15-1631 and '41-841, et seq., The Arizona Antiquities Act
General Policy Revision Dates: 6/91 Page 3
Rev. 5/00

19. "Principal investigator" means the person with overall administrative responsibility for a project.

20. "Project director" means the person immediately in charge of directing all phases of a project.

21. "Public repository" or "repository" means an institution that permanently houses and provides curatorial services for scientific or historical collections and records for the benefit of the public.

22. "Survey" means an activity with the purpose of locating, identifying and evaluating archaeological or paleontological sites without causing and disturbance of the ground.

B. General Coverage

1. The Rules and Regulations set forth in this Section shall be applicable to all persons, institutions,

organizations, or corporations who seek to undertake those activities set forth in A.R.S. '41-841.

2. No person, institution, organization, or corporation shall undertake any activity prescribed in A.R.S. '41-841 until a permit is first secured from the Director of the Arizona State Museum.

3. Disclaimer: There could be updates to this law that are not recorded here.

E18

About the author

Aaron Werner is the father of two beautiful children and lives in Utah with his talented wife, Angela. He has always been interested in the legendary stories of the monumental migration of the US population as it moved west and built a new society in the land that once belonged to the Native Americans. So many stories of adventure have disappeared and were never recorded, or are only known through old diaries and letters kept throughout the years. His hobby has been to discover the legends and attempt to separate those that are only folklore from those that are true. In his other job, he has been involved with internet technology and project development for over 20+ years, experience that has helped him to hone his research abilities.

Books by co-author Linda Gatewood:

The Winter Secret Series:

Winter Secret

Spring Promise

Summer Truth

Autumn Hush

A Chance to Remember

The Ghost of Fountain Courts

Timely Rendezvous

Available on Amazon.com

Made in the USA
Monee, IL
08 September 2024